"[A] splenetic wonder. . . . For all of its rousing, air-clearing invective, *The Whore of Akron* is strangely celebratory, making a particularly Jewish-American case for family and place, and for waiting and hoping past the point of reason. In Scott Raab's cosmos, where championship seasons seem about as likely as the arrival of the messiah, next year in Jerusalem might as well be next year in Cleveland. He suggests that there is nevertheless redemption to be had in grinding away at life, at parenthood, at work, and in loving something more than yourself until that longed-for day when victory arrives. Or doesn't. Don't hold a gaudy festival of self and flee to Miami, for instance. Stay in Cleveland and suffer." —Will Blythe, *New York Magazine*

"In pursuing James pre- and post-'Decision' . . . the author never does complete the subtitle's mission to find James' soul. Instead, Raab . . . discovers his own. And, in some twisted sense, maybe ours, too." —*Cleveland Plain Dealer*

"Visceral and raucously funny. . . . Perhaps the best book ever written about the ragged world of sports obsession. . . . Raab recounts, with electrifying insight, past and present instances of remorse, reconciliation, relapse, revulsion and, inevitably, a dare-not-to-mention-too-loud longing for simply the possibility of redemption." —*The Cleveland Leader*

"Spellbinding. . . . Compelling. . . . Gleefully vulgar. . . . Raab does not merely insert himself [into the narrative], he envelops it. *The Whore of Akron* bears little resemblance to any sports book I've ever read. It is far more similar to Charles Bukowski's *Hollywood* than anything David Halberstam or John Feinstein has ever written." —*Cavs: The Blog*

"*The Whore of Akron* is hilarious, heartfelt, and wincingly honest. This is the best kind of book, one that surprises."
—Buzz Bissinger, author of *Friday Night Lights* and coauthor of *Shooting Stars* (with LeBron James)

"With all due respect to Frederick Exley, Scott Raab has just written the smartest, funniest, most passionate, loving, hateful, bathetic, honest, and deeply personal sports jeremiad slash memoir of our time. Yeah, the guy doesn't like LeBron James. Not the point. *The Whore of Akron* is about a basketball player the way Moby-Dick is about a whale."
—Stefan Fatsis, author of *Word freak* and *A Few Seconds of Panic*

"Mr. Raab sure-footedly turns his monolithic hatred for Mr. James and devotion to Cleveland into a vehicle for exploring his struggles with drugs and alcohol, the mental illness and abandonment that have haunted his family, questions of faith and Jewish identity, and the joy of fatherhood." —*Wall Street Journal*

"*The Whore of Akron* isn't really about basketball. It's about addiction and sobriety, marriage and divorce, childhood and parenthood, loyalty and autonomy." —Theawl.com

"A searing manifesto that is impressively pointed and, in the end, even feels fair—not balanced, of course, but justified. . . . Whether you're convinced [of LBJ's treachery] depends not on whether you care about Cleveland sports, but if you care about sports at all. . . . Hilarious invective and smart commentary." —*Fortune*

"Hilarious." —*Christian Science Monitor*

"There is more passion, anger, and sublime writing in Scott Raab's *The Whore of Akron* than any fifty other books you'll read this (or any other year) combined." —*New York Post*

"A hilarious and profane love letter to fandom, faith, loyalty, and sports in America." —*Parade* magazine

"Genius. . . . Raab is Hunter S. Thompson, Wolfe, and Breslin; every bit as messed up, alienated, angry, bitchy, cruel, and angelic. . . . *The Whore of Akron* is a masterpiece."
—Dan Klores, *Huffington Post*

"A modern-day Portnoy's *Complaint*. Standing in for the piece of liver is LeBron James." —*Slate*

"As far as I know, a LeBron James is a hat worn by men in the 1920s." —Philip Roth

THE WHORE OF AKRON

THE
WHORE
OF
AKRON

ONE MAN'S SEARCH FOR
THE SOUL OF LEBRON JAMES

SCOTT RAAB

HARPER ⬤ PERENNIAL

NEW YORK • LONDON • TORONTO • SYDNEY • NEW DELHI • AUCKLAND

HARPER ● PERENNIAL

FIRST HARPER PERENNIAL EDITION PUBLISHED 2012.

Designed by William Ruoto

Library of Congress Cataloging-in-Publication Data has been applied for.

ISBN 978-0-06-206637-4

12 13 14 15 16   OV/RRD   10 9 8 7 6 5 4 3 2 1

To Lisa, Judah, and Pip

CONTENTS

And there followed another angel, saying,

Babylon is fallen, is fallen, that great city,

because she made all nations drink of the wine

of the wrath of her fornication.

—REVELATION 14:8

All men are Jews, except they don't know it.

—BERNARD MALAMUD

THE WHORE OF AKRON

CHAPTER ONE

INTIMATIONS

I no more chose to be a Clevelander and a Cleveland fan than I chose to be a Jew transfixed by leggy *shiksas*. It is my birthright, my legacy, my destiny. My fate was cast in 1964 on a Sunday afternoon at Cleveland Municipal Stadium, while Canadian gusts swept across Lake Erie and through the mammoth double-decked bowl in damp, endless circles cold enough to stiffen snot. I have seen Paris at dusk; I have prayed at the Wailing Wall; I have beheld the twin scoops of Rebecca Romijn's vanilla ass: yet never have I been so transported, never so ecstatic, as on December 27, 1964, when the Cleveland Browns beat the Baltimore Colts and won the NFL World Championship.

I was twelve years old. Old enough to stand fast, amid men warmed by whiskey and their fiery love for the Browns, and drink in the sight of 80,000 of our number rising as the clock ticked toward infinity, fixing that victory forever as a fact of history, past insult or dispute. That flag still flies in my soul. The roar still echoes in my ears. The vision—of Cleveland triumphant, of Cleveland fans in communal thrall to a joy beyond all words, of a Cleveland team lifting the town's immortal heart to heaven—still fills my eyes. I'm fifty-nine years old now, far from Cleveland in every way save one: I still live with the Browns, the Indians, the Cavaliers, and I will die with them. They were a solace and source of hope when I had no other reason to wake up, and now that I am a man—the father of a twelve-year-old, the husband of a leggy *shiksa*, a sober alcoholic and drug-free addict—those teams remain a psychic rock, an anchor for my wobbling, fretful soul. Unlike two entire generations of Cleveland fans who have grown up rooting for Cleveland teams and have tasted only defeat and despair, I know what it feels like to win it all. And I have waited forty-seven years to feel it one last time before I go.

LAST TIME I spoke to LeBron James, he was wearing a towel in the Cavs locker room at Quicken Loans Arena. The nightly media scrum wedged tight around his double-wide had retreated to their laptops to file their stories. The Cavs had won without playing particularly well, but it was April 2010, the end of another long regular season; the Cavaliers were 60–16 and already had secured home-court advantage through the playoffs.

They were an extraordinary team: led by LeBron, the league's best player, in the prime of his prime. The Cavs sold out every time and everywhere they played. Led by LeBron, they were known around the globe. Led by LeBron, they were the best thing to have happened to Cleveland—*all* of Cleveland, black and white, young and old, East Side and West—since Jim Brown walked away from the NFL in 1965.

Led by LeBron. Who was our native son. Who had become the face not just of Cleveland, but of all Ohio. Who was about to win his second MVP award in a row.

Who was shortly to become a free agent. Who palmed our collective fate in one huge hand.

In a league full of athletes whose bodies can honestly be described as beautiful—one of the aesthetic delights of an NBA locker room is watching from a distance as the pack of mainly fat, mainly white members of the press gathers and ungathers itself as each chiseled specimen emerges from the shower—LeBron James is a masterpiece. Hewn of sinew, apparently impervious as iron—muscled yet sleek, thick-shouldered yet loose of limb, James looks different from every other player in the league, especially in a damp towel.

Still, there's nothing especially forbidding about a guy in a towel, even LeBron. He's a kid who just took a shower, and the fact that he can do things that I can only dream of—the physical summit of my day is a decent bowel movement—doesn't change that. Besides, I'd been following the Cavs all season, and while I wasn't sure James knew my name, we'd spoken in passing a few times. He had withdrawn from any media contact to avoid questions about his impending free agency—the five-minute post-game scrums were the sum total of his availability, and asking about free agency was itself off-limits—but he sometimes was willing to field a question if you sidled up after the pack departed.

I had no question to ask. I was heading back home to New Jersey from the arena, but I knew that the next time I saw him would be during the playoffs—crazy time—and I felt I had to speak my piece. I had seen him come into the NBA at age eighteen and, from his first game forward, outplay all the absurd hype around him. I had watched grown men, league stalwarts, shuffle out of his way as he drove to the rim. I had laughed as teammates were hit in the head by bullet passes they hadn't dreamed James could thread through a web of defenders. And I had sat in a hotel room in Hollywood on May 31, 2007, alone, awestruck, and weeping as he scored the Cavs' last 25 points and destroyed the Detroit Pistons in a double-overtime playoff victory, the single most astonishing performance by any Cleveland athlete I've ever seen. I had studied him closely and been dazzled a thousand times and more. No other way to put it: it is an honor and privilege just to watch this motherfucker play.

"I *saw* Oscar in his prime." I told him. "Michael. Magic. *All* of them. And you're the best basketball player I've *ever* seen. Thank you."

I did and do not intend to degrade Oscar Robertson or Michael Jordan or anyone else. Nor am I claiming any kind of objectivity: I'm a native Clevelander and a Cavs fan since 1970, the year of their birth. Yeah, I know: count the rings. But I'm not talking about rings; I'm talking about pure *game*. All I'm saying is LeBron James is the best fucking basketball player I've ever seen.

He savored my little speech for a second or two, smiling ear to ear, eyes bright.

"That means a lot to me," he said, utterly sincere. "Thanks."

That was it. I didn't urge him to stick around, to stay with the Cavs and become the Moses every Cleveland fan felt he'd be. It didn't occur to me. Everyone—even the most cynical out-of-town beat reporter—assumed that LeBron was going to re-sign with the Cavs for at least three more years. Northeast Ohio was his home; Dan Gilbert, the Cavs owner, spent freely to get players to complement his game; adoring fans filled the Q every night, thousands of them clad in replicas of his jersey like it was the Shroud of Turin.

Trust me: I'm not sorry I didn't say any of that, and I'm certainly not silly enough to believe that anything I could've said would've meant diddly. Which isn't to say that I have no regrets about that conversation. I feel, in fact, a deep and abiding sense of regret—I say this as a man who has known the pain of divorce, not to mention as a Jew who bought a hundred shares of Apple at seventeen and sold them all at twenty-two—I feel remorse unto grief about that night in the locker room with LeBron.

I'm sorry, truly sorry, that I didn't haul off and kick him square in the nuts.

EVERY MAN HAS a mission, a calling, a higher purpose, and if he lives long enough, life itself will thrust that mission upon him. Not in a moment of blinding insight—literature aside, the sole epiphany in life is that life offers no epiphanies—but rather as erosion. Surfaces wear away; the center crumbles; the things that once seemed vital prove their essential meaninglessness as the years go by, and what's left—what is finally *revealed*—turns out to be the reason God breathed life into our very soul.

My mission is to bear witness. I've done that for many years now, most of them writing for *Esquire* magazine. I've borne witness to all kinds of stuff, dumb and otherwise. I've shared cunnilingus tips with Robert Downey Jr.; I got tattoos with Dennis Rodman; I once smoked a bone with Tupac, twice did nothing with Larry David, and visited with Phil Spector in his castle in Alhambra three times, all without gun-play. I've written about drug-addled anesthesiologists, AIDS-stricken pedophiles, and Holocaust death-camp guards. Hell, I even went to Bill Murray's house once for an Oscar party.

None of that felt anything like a mission; it felt like the sweetest job in journalism, the best gig any writer could ever have. I spent years selling shoes, tending bar, dealing drugs, and worse; my last time card was punched in 1983 at a nursing home where part of my job was to clean and dress old men in the morning; if one died in the middle of the night, I helped the funeral-home driver load the corpse. I've kept the time card; I was thirty-one years old when I left that job, and I've taken nothing for granted since.

This is different; this is no mere job. Like all worthy missions, mine is far simpler to state than to accomplish.

Bearing witness. To Cleveland. To the faith, hope, and hunger that bind the soul of a people to their home. To the transcendental glory of sport and its spirit, fierce and pure, beyond corruption, that drives grown men to whisper to their sons, "I saw it with my own eyes. I was *there.*" To LeBron, who once seemed to embody that soul, and then betrayed it. And, above all, to the Cleveland fans, the veritable nation of Job, whose love burns yet through all the heartache and scorn.

KING JAMES. THE Chosen One. The Whore of Akron. I dropped that last one on him myself, after he left to join the Miami Heat. For seven years, LeBron did the same thing as any trollop worth her taxi fare: he made the right noises, told us how good it felt, how big we were, how he loved us, how special we were. He never even told us not to touch his hair.

Oh, we knew—some of us knew better than others, of course—that he was only a child, and a child born unto a hapless mother more or less a child herself. His vast sense of childish entitlement seemed to speak louder every season. But, lord, the sex was fine. And there was very little he wouldn't or couldn't do; he'd even play in the low post once in a while. Good as he was from the get-go, he got better each time around. LeBron James put out like no one else.

"WE ARE ALL WITNESSES" is what the 10-story Nike banner in downtown Cleveland said, but that was just slick copywriting. The fans' relationship was deeper, more complex; the hard part of bearing witness to LeBron James has little to do with him as an athlete, and everything to do with what it means to be a Cleveland fan. When he wore a Yankees cap to Jacobs Field for the opener of a playoff series between the Tribe and the Yankees in 2007—and was interviewed during the game on national television, still wearing the cap—I wrote him off as worthless scum.

"The sooner this son of a bitch hauls his ass out of Ohio, the better," to be exact.

I caught a ton of nasty shit for that, all from Clevelanders too young ever to have seen any Cleveland team win a title in any pro sport. I tried to explain to a few of them that the issue wasn't that James had grown up a fucking Yankees fan; the problem was how indifferent he appeared while insulting Cleveland and the fans who worshipped him—and who paid to watch him play.

Take Larry Bird, I'd say. If young Larry had worn a fucking Yankees cap to the opener of a playoff series between the Red Sox and the fucking Yankees, it's no stretch to say that it would've had a severe and lasting impact on his career as a Celtic. Red Auerbach would've had Bird in hand at a press conference the next day to apologize to all of New England, but Bird still would've been mistrusted for the rest of his days in Boston. And rightly so.

This meant absolutely nothing to any Cleveland fans. Not because they didn't love Cleveland and the Cavaliers and Browns and Indians, but because they weren't old enough to have known Cleveland when Cleveland felt any collective pride and dignity. Having lived their whole lives in a punch line, having watched their favorite ballplayers leave as free agents or in lopsided trades, having seen each local franchise build a team seemingly good enough to win it all but doomed to fail in the end, often under circumstances so absurdly painful that some of them came to believe the town was actually cursed: Pride and dignity were foreign to a fan base whose daily bread had forever tasted of ash.

LeBron was their hero, their sole hope for a redemption they had yearned for all their lives but dimly understood. Traumatized by the Browns' departure in 1995 and frustrated by the ongoing ineptitude of the neo-Browns; haunted by the ultimate failures of the Indians' great mid- and late 1990s teams; condemned forever to viewing pre-game montages of past disasters—The Catch, The Shot, The Drive, The Fumble—each time a Cleveland team made it to a playoff game: little wonder they were King James's happily abject serfs.

The Yankees cap was too much. I gave up—gave up trying to explain, trying to convince them that they didn't know what they didn't know; gave up, too, on James and the Cavs. My eight-year-old son, God bless him, tossed his LeBron jersey into the trash can, and I boycotted the entire 2008 season. I couldn't bring myself to care about a team led by a player who cared nothing for the fans and the town. I had left Cleveland in 1984—I was not some schmuck doomed to failure and disgrace. Not me—no fucking way.

But I hadn't yet grasped the mission. I didn't understand my debt to Cleveland and to the teams who formed and inspired me, who gave me a place in the world and a purpose for being when nothing was all I had.

I STILL HAVE my ticket stub from 12/27/64. Section 7, Row Z, Seat 19, one of my uncle Manny's season tickets, lower deck, on the 50-yard line, last row. The upper deck cut off the top of punts, but the view of all the drunks listing as they staggered up and down the narrow walkways to void their bladders at the men's room trough was compensation enough.

"Let's go, Brownies," they'd chant, and the black-eyed pea of my heart sang along with them. I was stuck at the bottom of my young life. I came from what they once called a "broken" home. We'd moved from Cleveland to Los Angeles in 1960; my parents split up in 1963 and my mom—a thirty-three-year-old waif with three sons, no marketable skills, no college degree, and no love for the goyische San Fernando Valley—moved us back to Cleveland and into her parents' house.

We weren't the Waltons. There were seven of us at first, including my great-grandmother, who was wise enough to die a week after we moved in. That left my mother, her three sons, and my grandparents—Orthodox Jewish immigrants who spoke Yiddish and often went at each other like gut-shot bears until the cops came to settle things down. My grandfather no doubt was holding back—a laborer retired from the New York Central Railroad, he was a miserably failed writer and painter, batshit crazy to boot, who long ago had built himself a cell of his own in the basement and rarely emerged. Gram, with a pipe fitter's arms and hands so thickly calloused she could grab a tray of kugel hot from the oven without any mitt or dish towel, never called him by any name but Ipish—"stench"—and she'd hack at him with a big kitchen broom like Teddy fucking Williams taking BP.

I went a little nuts, too. My philandering father was thousands of miles away, and my mother was more focused on her martyrdom than motherhood. She never tired of telling me what a bastard my father was and how little he cared about us, and I was pissed off about the whole deal. As the oldest, I beat my brothers as often as possible.

Once, my brother David and I tried to kill the old man. While he was at *shul*, we wedged the front and side doors tight, waited on the upstairs back porch until he came around to the back door, and then fired every knife in the house down at him in hope of poleaxing his yarmulked skull with one of them.

Month after month and year after year this went on, and nobody did anything about any of it. People felt sorry for us, which enraged me. I can imagine no firmer basis for shame and anger than to be a mere object of pity. My mother would come home from the only job she could find, as a doctor's receptionist, and scream at her mother for having fed us. "We're going to eat like a *family*," my mother would shriek, and so we'd eat a second dinner. My grades were awful. I was getting fatter and fatter; the only bathroom was upstairs, and so my grandmother would put an empty coffee can at the base of the stairs for us to piss in, to spare us the hike. It never occurred to these numbskulls that maybe I needed something more than four meals a day.

Ah, well. There were neither boundaries nor consequences, perfect training for a writer. I read, wrote, and ate compulsively, still several years away from staggering up the long walkway of my own alcoholism and addiction. I was sullen and alone in the world, my hopelessness matched only by my waistline and my rage.

But I had an uncle—Manny Dolin, God rest his soul—an electrical contractor who spent more time in Las Vegas and bankruptcy court than he did working. But Manny owned season tickets, and so I had the Browns. And the Browns had Jimmy Brown, the best football player in the NFL; and a brilliant mathematician at quarterback, Frank Ryan; and the smartest owner in the whole world, Arthur B. Modell, an adman from Brooklyn, a Jew so shrewd that he'd managed to buy the best franchise in football with a mere $250,000 of his own loot. Even after he shitcanned Paul Brown, gridiron genius and the man for whom the team was named, Modell rode a wave of popularity—at least on the East Side, where all of Cleveland's Jews lived—until his slow metamorphosis turned him into a cross between Shylock and Bernie Madoff, a vile creature whose insatiable greed and want of anything like integrity led him to steal the team away from Cleveland. May he suffer another decade of strokes and spend eternity tonguing Satan's flaming anus.

On December 27, 1964, Manny was in Miami Beach where he spent two weeks late each winter, so Uncle Lorry picked me up and we headed downtown. Lorry drove a Country Squire, a Ford station wagon, and drove it steady—like a pharmacist, which is exactly what he was. Manny drove a Buick Electra 225 the yellow of banana cream pie, screaming from stop light to stop light a hundred blocks down Chester Avenue while butchering Sinatra in a voice grated by two packs of Pall Malls a day; Lorry didn't smoke or sing, but he hit each light the instant it turned green. It felt like an omen, and it was. We parked and walked down West 3rd Street, into the teeth of the wind. The day was dark gray at one p.m., the lake and sky one seamless horizon that seemed to start just above our heads, the sidewalk a sea of men in topcoats and dress hats and earmuffs, an army fueled by the flasks in their coats' inside pockets, shuffling toward Gate A, toward triumph and glory eternal.

I KNOW: I understand how lame, how hollow, how bathetic all that may seem. It didn't feel that way to me then; it doesn't now. When I Google "W. 3rd St., Cleveland" and see those men frozen forever, mostly dead now but younger that Sunday than I am today, my throat aches and my eyes fill with tears.

I know: it's only a game. But what a game. The Colts were 7-point favorites, on the road. Coached by thirty-four-year-old Don Shula—drafted by the Browns after going to college in Cleveland—they boasted the league's best offense, with six future Hall of Famers, led by Johnny U at quarterback—*and* the NFL's best defense. But Unitas threw two picks into the wind, Dr. Ryan tossed three TDs, and Jim Brown gained 114 yards. The Browns won, 27–0.

The official attendance that day was 79,544, and not one of them would've believed that he'd never live to see another Cleveland team win a championship.

The Cuyahoga River catching fire?

Maybe.

Fish by the thousands washing up dead on Lake Erie's shore?

Possible.

Cleveland a national joke?

Not bloody likely.

But the notion that generation after generation of Cleveland fans could be born and grow old and die without celebrating a title?

Get the fuck *outa here.*

I was there. I saw it happen. It gave me an abiding sense of faith—in my town and its teams—that will never fade, that no amount of hurt and heartbreak can destroy. All those fucking Yankees fans are absolutely right. Flags fly forever. *Forever.*

SPAKE THE WHORE of Akron in his first major print interview after The Decision:

"Maybe the ones burning my jersey were never LeBron fans anyway."

Exactamente, you megalomaniacal shitheel. Those were—they are—*Cleveland* fans. They burned their jerseys right after your hour-long ESPN smarm fest, when the whole world saw you for the stunted, soul-dead bumpkin you are. Those Cleveland fans knew for the first time what utter fools they had been to believe that LeBron James ever gave a damn about anything *but* LeBron James.

And because they were born and grew up and will die Cleveland fans, those fans also instantly grasped your legacy as a Cavalier: You will forever be the player who choked and quit against the Celtics in the 2009–2010 playoffs. You surrendered. You gave up. You and your team—while the clock still ran, with the coach urging you on—quit trying, laid down and died.

For that disgrace alone, those fans were right to burn the stinking jerseys they themselves had paid for. Add the disdain and the disrespect you showed for Cleveland as Jim Gray and Michael Wilbon fellated you on national TV—not a single question about your playoff tank job or the phantom elbow injury that floated in the same ether as the rumors of your mother's sexual dalliance with one of your teammates—hell, those fans should have torched those jerseys with you and your sycophant posse wearing them.

·   ·   ·

WHEN THE CAVALIERS were born in October 1970, I was a college freshman, a 275-pound *bulvan*, and a blackout drunk. I never drank in high school. I never went out on a date or to a party or dance. I ate and I slept and I tried not to murder my mother, who never stopped screaming at me, or my brother Dave, who was much quieter. I punched him instead of my mother because I knew that if I ever punched my mother, I wouldn't stop until she was dead.

A C+ high school student with good SAT scores, I went to Case Western Reserve University because they gave me financial aid, a work-study job, and room and board in a dorm where I'd never have to hear Lucille's voice again. The dorm was eight floors of freshmen, many of them Jewboys from New York City and North Jersey who'd missed the cut at the Ivies and whose folks could afford to send them to CWRU, which had more cachet than a state college. They came with treasure—marijuana, pills, and tabs of acid; Zappa, Dylan, and the Velvet Underground; *Zap Comix*, the *National Lampoon*, and Bukowski.

It didn't matter that I was scared to talk to a girl or that I felt imprisoned by fat or that I stole because I had no money. All of that stuff went away. I washed down reds with Mad Dog, dropped acid, smoked weed around the clock, and made friends.

By the end of my first semester, I stopped doing anything but drugs, and my closest buddy was Big George, a huge young black man I met at breakfast one morning at

Leutner Commons, where I'd line up at six a.m. and eat plate after plate of hash browns. Like me, he was a local kid, but from the Glenville ghetto. I don't even know if he was a student.

George took a shine to me because I didn't give a shit about anything but getting fucked up and eating. There was nowhere I wouldn't go, nothing I wouldn't do. I'd ride with him into Glenville off East 105th to deliver tin-foil packets of heroin to men who'd scarcely look up from their card games at the hulking white boy who barely came up to George's shoulder.

I never shot heroin, not that anyone offered. Never saw George shoot up, either. I didn't handle the cash or carry a piece. I was there to learn to play Tonk and listen to them "aw-c'mon-baby" their women on the phone. I was there to ogle their orange shag carpet and breathe in their musk. I was there because I had nowhere else to be until three or four a.m., when George and I would head back to Case and start cracking the dorm vending machines. I was there because I came from a paternal line of Jews who weren't doctors or lawyers.

There was one doctor, actually. My father's uncle Julius performed abortions on Jewish girls and then served hard federal time and lost his medical license after pleading to income-tax evasion. Papa Juicy adopted my old man during the Great Depression, after my real grandfather—a trumbenik named Willie, a bum out of Belz, Ukraine, a bigamist and a bagman and bomb-roller for the Cleveland Syndicate during the Laundry Wars—left his wife and five kids to starve. It was Julius, Russian-born, who changed Rabinowitz to Raab.

My father grew up believing that his own mother, Julius's sister, had sold him to Julius. *Sold* him. Why *not* believe it? Where my father grew up, off Kinsman Road, the Jews were dirt-poor, hard as nails. There were no scholars, only junkmen. Two of my father's sisters turned tricks for small change, food, and clothes, while his mother, Gussie, sat on her bed all day, weeping. Julius was a prick—I got to know him well—but Julius had money.

My father, who years later studied law and passed the California bar in his forties, then sank for the first time into a depression so crippling that he never again attempted to practice. He got a call one day from a sister who told him that Willie was dying in New York and wanted to see him.

Fuck him, my father said. Fuck him.

I knew none of this when I was running with Big George. I didn't know that I was embracing my heritage. I didn't grow up with my father around, didn't know Willie ever walked the earth, didn't know why I couldn't wait to kill somebody. Anybody. If some student or janitor had ever walked into the basement of a dorm where George and I were prying open a candy or cigarette machine, I would've skulled him with a crowbar, smiling.

I was happy then. I was building something. A bridge connecting me to the world. A fortress where I could stay untouched and untouchable. A battering ram I'd use to crash through my fear of being a lousy writer, which is what I was.

Whatever else I was building, though, mainly I was digging a tunnel. For twenty-five years I dug like a motherfucker; facing a life sentence as me without parole, I dug and dug and dug. I was strong as an ox, and, in my way, innocent, a big lout who'd rather steal than work, a fat virgin during a time of free love who was afraid of women and couldn't imagine why any female would want anything to do with him.

And there was nothing in the world I loved more than grabbing the Windermere bus west from University Circle down Euclid Avenue to 37th Street and watch those infant Cavs trying to imitate an NBA team.

OBVIOUSLY, I MYSELF don't know or care how or where to draw a line between fan and fanatic. Hooligan, shmooligan: I'm not talking about thuggery or booze-fueled violence in the grandstand; I mean the sort of ardor and passion that soccer fans around the globe bring to the World Cup. You don't get to decide if you're born in Uruguay and you turn out to be the best *fútbol* player on the planet, and you are possessed of even a shred of sanity, that you'd rather play for Argentina in the Cup, and then lay claim to victim status when the citizens of Uruguay hang you, in effigy or not, as a traitor.

I acknowledge the validity of the view that fanhood is a matter of rooting for laundry, that the names on the back of the jersey will change as the years go by, and that loyalty—the word tattooed in cursive script running up LeBron's left rib cage—is not integral to the business of pro sports. It's a one-way street stretching from the fan to the franchise and its players.

Fans see their teams as quasi–public utilities and the players as hometown heroes. A major league franchise treats its fans as a vast herd of cash cows who must be milked for the money to pay for everything from ticket-service fees to the bond issues that funnel tax dollars to the billionaire owners to help build their play palaces. Any Cleveland fan who believes otherwise should've left for Baltimore with Art Modell, may his testicles wither as his tongue swells to the girth of an eggplant.

As for the players, they function essentially as movie stars did when Hollywood was run by a handful of studios. In exchange for fame and fortune, their services are owned by a small industry that functions as a monopoly and generates billions of dollars in revenue streams not only for the NBA itself, but also for related industries, such as media and apparel. They have a union, which is a poodle among pit bulls. They have a narrow window of opportunity to make stupid money—a window that starts closing as soon as they enter the NBA—and they risk career-ending injury each time they take the floor. To top it off, fans demand that players embrace forever the home team and town, forsaking all others till death, retirement, or suckitude ensues, in which case they essentially cease to exist.

It's as nasty a business as any other. I get it. Cleveland fans get it. The next Cleveland sports hero who reaches free agency and opts to stay will be the first of his kind. Likewise the next free-agent superstar from elsewhere who signs with a Cleveland team . . . it never, ever shakes out that way, because the young, glamorous, and gifted don't want to come to Cleveland. The weather is rugged. The economy is rugged. The women are rugged. For a young millionaire not named Bruce Wayne, the art museum and symphony don't matter. The Cleveland Clinic doesn't matter. The grit and guts that are supposed to make the underdog beloved don't matter, either.

What made LeBron James matter so much—what made his coming to the Cavs seem like a miraculous twist of fate—was that he understood all of this and more. His pride in being a son of this soil was our own pride; his history, too, was ours. He hungered, like all of us, for affirmation and respect. He could rewrite our history and restore our pride and finally, after half a century, make *us* matter.

In the end, what truly matters is this: Cleveland fans love the city, cherish the teams more deeply, and pull for them with far more passion than fans anywhere else. Other Rust Belt cities have been stripped of a middle class over the past fifty years by the same socioeconomic Katrina, but only Cleveland became the armpit of a nation.

Detroit is a sinkhole of permanent despair, Pittsburgh's a human sewer, but fans in those cities know at least what victory looks, sounds, and feels like, and they limp a little taller and stink slightly less for that knowledge.

That's why I hung on to that stub from 1964, while I smoked, snorted, drank, lost, or sold everything else that had meant anything to me. I never thought of it as a talisman or souvenir. It was *evidence*, not that I had been there, but that Cleveland had.

WHEN I BEGAN to follow the Cavs, hoping to write a book about how LeBron James led them and every Cleveland fan in creation to the Promised Land at last, I dug the ticket stub out of a small box in the attic, dropped it into a Ziploc bag, and brought it with me whenever I headed to Cleveland. It was a sales tool—I wanted the Cavaliers to know that I was a lifer who had seen the franchise born, back when tickets to see them play at the old Cleveland Arena cost a buck with a student ID, a few cents less than a pint of Mad Dog—and it was an ideal conversation starter.

So it was that on Tuesday, January 19, 2010, when I spotted Jim Brown himself hobbling down the hallway deep in the bowels of the Q, I was able to pull the stub from my bag as I walked up to him.

Even at age seventy-three, bent on a cane and wrapped into a dark blue suit, Brown exudes a barely veiled ferocity. With eyes set deep into a cannonball skull, his gaze feels like a glare. He does not smile easily or often. His mustache is a coiled muscle that looks like it could lead the league in rushing.

You can debate all night about the greatest running back ever, but you'll never find another athlete in any sport who stands as tall—both as an on-field force and as an archetype of American manhood—as Jim Brown. He stood up to Paul Brown as a young star when all his teammates warned him to tuck his tail. He spoke and wrote with insight and a cold fury about civil rights back in 1964, and retired to make movies at age twenty-nine, in response to being fined and bullied by his owner, Art Modell—may he be buried naked in a pigsty with a corncob wedged in every orifice.

"I wanted to show this to you," I said, handing him the ticket stub. "You're the only other guy in Cleveland who I'm *sure* was there that day."

Brown grunted as he held it up and cocked his head to get a closer look. "Cool," he said.

"I was twelve years old," I told him. "I'll never forget it. But I never thought I'd have to wait another forty-six years."

Brown squinted at me, genuinely puzzled.

"Another forty-six years for what?"

It hit me with considerable force, that question. He truly didn't know. And why should he? He *won* that ring, went out on top, and lives forever—and stays forever young—within the ebbing, fatty hearts of ancient

Clevelanders. He never was a fan. He's Jim fucking Brown.

LeBron James was waiting down the hall and around the corner—in sweatpants and a gray T-shirt—along with a pack of media hounds. It was the day after Martin Luther King Jr. Day and the kickoff of the Cavs' "Black Heritage Month."

Thus did the Whore of Akron, showing all his gleaming teeth, greet Jim Brown:

"What's up, legend?"

They took turns signing a blown-up *Sports Illustrated* cover—"Lakeside Legends"—produced for the occasion. James told the media he would have a copy framed for himself.

"I want it to be legendary," said LeBron James. "Anytime you can be mentioned with a great and be able to continue the legacy he built in Cleveland is humbling for me. Being from the younger generation and seeing everything he did for the city of Cleveland was awesome. We both know how much the fans love sports. Being a Clevelander, being from this area, I've had to learn to keep the momentum going after he passed the torch."

The torch, yes. You're going to need that fucking torch, pally. It's going to come in handy down in Dante's ninth circle of Hell—at the very bottom—where the worst of sinners are encased in ice for the worst of human crimes: treachery.

CHAPTER TWO

THE HANDSHAKE
AND
THE HANDJOB

forgave the bastard his Yankees cap in April 2009. It was during the week of Passover, which has nothing to do with forgiveness, except that I called my cousin Jeff to wish him a good Pesach, and he asked whether I was still upset about the cap enough to keep boycotting the Cavs.

Fuck, yeah. I'd track them online and I'd catch game highlights on ESPN, but no League Pass and no tuning in when they were on TV, which by then was twice a week, because they had LeBron and were a juggernaut.

"Just watch them," Jeff said. "They have a shot at going all the way."

"You sound serious."

"I am serious."

This was significant, a complete departure from the standard of fearful gloom endemic to both the average Cleveland fan and the average Jew. Jeff had been a Cavs season-ticket holder since LeBron's second season, but he was no optimist, despite having grown up in Shaker Heights apparently free of any crippling neurosis beyond a profound dread of airplane travel and a burgeoning love of whales. He knew in his bones that neither a season of hope for a Cleveland team nor life itself was fated to end with the sort of parade where happy crowds line the sidewalks, cheering. If Jeff was talking title, I was listening.

I watched them play the Celtics that Sunday, April 12.

The Cavs were still battling the Lakers for the league's best record, which would give them home-court advantage through the playoffs, and the Celtics needed one more win to clinch the second seed in the conference. But they were without Kevin Garnett, who was injured, and the game was in Cleveland. It figured to be a win for the Cavs.

It was much sweeter than that. Boston was meat by the end of the first quarter, which ended with the Cavs ahead, 31–9. James scored 29 in 30 minutes, but what made me hard had zip to do with him. I saw Mo Williams and Delonte West playing with James like they had come up together on the same AAU squad, I saw the Cavaliers hunker down on defense as if their girlfriends' babies' lives depended on getting stops—Paul Pierce and Ray Allen shot a combined 6–25—and I saw the rarest and most precious of all things: a Cleveland team with a killer's instinct. From the tip, they stomped the living shit out of Boston.

I called Jeff after the game, just to cackle. *What the fuck*: I'm in. I'm down for the whole playoff run, and if they get to the Finals, I'm there in person. I don't care how much I have to pay; need be, I'll tap the kid's 529. Los Angeles, Denver, San Antonio: wherever this leads—I am *there*.

Call me a front-runner, a bandwagon jumper, a glory hound. I know my own fan's heart, and that fan's heart is pure. I didn't tell myself that LeBron had changed somehow, but he was playing better than he ever had, and the whole team seemed bound by an *esprit*, an honest joy.

Much of it—the pre-game mime shows and handshake routines, the half-court underhand-shot attempts, and the ritual tossing of chalk at the scorer's table—was sophomoric nonsense raised to the level of pregame ritual: LeBron James was all of twenty-four years old, the ultimate local boy made good. He had grown up playing with the same group of guys from age eight on; his teammates had been his best friends, his family, his soul mates. Now he was the alpha dog on the NBA's best team and striving to re-create that brotherhood.

And maybe, just maybe, he'd grown up some, too. Moses, after all, took forever to get his mind right enough to stutter-step all those poor Hebrews to the land of milk and honey.

A FUNNY THING happened along the glory trail, however: Mo Williams lost his jumper.

I want to say something pleasant here about Maurice Williams, a moon-faced Mississippian who has forged an NBA career despite entering the league as a second-round draft choice, despite standing barely six feet tall, and despite an apparently untreatable allergy to playing defense.

Mo loves dogs—he's a partner in a pit bull breeding business—and he worships the Mob. His *nom de hoops* is Mo Gotti, and the PA system at Quicken Loans Arena blares the refrain of the love theme from *The Godfather* when he sinks a three-pointer. It always makes me wonder if Mo

Williams grasps what a warm greeting he'd get were he to wander into the Ravenite Social Club to pay his respects.

Mo also has my favorite NBA tattoo, a fluffy cloud erratically inked on his upper back, in the vicinity of his right shoulder blade. Inside the cloud, the letters "NBA" sit stacked in block capitals, with each the first letter of another word:

> Never
> Broke
> Again

In short, Mo Williams is an innocent, an insecure yokel stamped forever by rurality and impoverishment.

Perhaps that helps explain why Mo is also a choker, unable to perform under playoff pressure. During the regular season, he was an All Star, second on the team behind LeBron in points and assists, and as one of the best 3-point shooters in the league, capable of picking up the scoring slack if LeBron needed a blow—and capable of keeping defenses honest and the lanes open for James to drive. But when Cleveland ran into trouble in the playoffs, Mo Williams screwed the pooch.

Streaky during the first two rounds, when it hardly mattered—the Cavs swept all eight games; none of them close—Mo fell to pieces versus Orlando in the Eastern Conference Finals. It wasn't just his numbers—although they were awful—it was his face, which bore the same tight-lipped tension as a crampy third-grader about to dump a load into his pants.

The Cavaliers lost the series opener, 107–106, at the Q, after building a 15-point lead at the half and with LeBron scoring 49 points. The loss didn't merely suck the wind out of the crowd, it ruined Mo Williams. After the game, LeBron sat at his locker, his face buried in his hands, while Mo whispered apologies with an arm over James's shoulders, vowing to do better.

With good reason: During the season, Mo was the Cavs' second option on offense. When teams double- and triple-teamed LeBron, the ball went to Williams. Against the Magic that night—Orlando collapsed on James and dared Mo to shoot—he missed six of eight 3-pointers and seven of his eleven other shots.

He got worse. James hit a last-second shot to win Game 2, 96–95; Williams missed five of six 3-pointers, and nine more shots overall. LeBron's game winner was a great moment in Cavalier history, a desperate, distant prayer that shook the arena and lifted me screaming off the couch, but the Magic hadn't played well, the Cavs had needed a miracle to win—and the next two games were in Florida.

Truth was, the Cavs were dead.

IN THE MIDDLE of the Orlando series, Joe Gabriele fell from the sky. He sent a question to *Esquire*'s Answer

Fella, the anonymous advice column I'd written for the magazine since 2000—"Is it illegal to flip off a cop, or just rude?"—and when I saw by his signature tag that he worked for the Cavs, I got in touch right away.

"If you get the chance," I wrote Joe, "tell Coach Mike to tell Mo that Answer Fella said . . . relax."

I posted that on Sunday morning, May 24. The Cavs lost that afternoon to go down 2–1. Mo Gotti missed seven of ten 3-pointers and shot 5–16 overall. LeBron scored 41 points, 18 of them on free throws. The Magic no longer bothered to defend Mo—nearly all of his shots were wide open looks—and James played most of the game with two or three defenders hanging from his torso.

Joe wrote back from Orlando two days later, just before Game 4's tip-off.

"When we get back to Cleveland, let me know. I'll get you a couple tix or a media pass to the game. If we make it to the Promised Land in June, same thing. In the meantime, keep the faith."

The Cavs took the floor that night and lost again—by 2 points, in overtime. LeBron scored 44; by this time, he was assembling one of the best playoff performances in league history—and Mo Gotti shot 5–15, missing all three of his 3-point attempts.

After my son left for school the next morning and my wife went upstairs to work, I sat a long time in the rocking chair in the living room, pondering whether I should bother going to Cleveland for Game 5.

What exactly was the nature of my faith?

Its depth I knew, or, rather, felt. My wife I love with all my heart, and I would take a bullet for my boy—but decades before I ever met Lisa or saw my son's face, I lived and died with Cleveland sports. Fanship was essential, a part of me without which I would not have known my soul.

My faith never was mild, and rarely pretty. In junior high, I was a regular caller to Pete Franklin, an early, nasty sports-talk radio avatar. At games, I was an angry jackass. In front of the TV, I was worse—a screaming, cursing asshole. All I wanted was the one thing that my teams always struggled to deliver: a win. In lieu of that, I wanted blood. And this—this wanting, this passion, this bottomless well of need and furious love—had become my living faith, an elemental way of defining life itself.

The truth that came to me that morning as I sat in the rocker dawned slow and shook me to the core. It was not a crumbling of my faith, which had fed upon a half century of season-ending defeats so naked in their bitterness that they had become national legend, a five-minute reel the networks ran whenever a Cleveland team made it to a big game.*

---

* It always begins with The Catch, when Willie Mays snared Vic Wertz's 420-foot drive in the eighth inning of Game 1 of the 1954 World Series. There were runners on first and second and no outs; the game was tied 2–2. The Giants won that game in the bottom of the tenth on a pop-fly home run down the right-field line and went on to sweep the Tribe—whose 111 regular-season wins that year stood as the major league record for another 44 years.

What shook me was the realization that a fundamental tenet of my faith—a Cleveland team would win another championship during my lifetime—might be wrong.

I began to cry. Quietly, at first. Followed by soft moaning. Soft, I say: I really didn't want my wife to hear me. But she did, and she came downstairs.

"What's *wrong*?"

"They can't beat Orlando," I said. "It isn't going to happen."

She came over to the chair and bent to hug me.

"I'm never going to see it," I sniffled. "Not even with LeBron."

"Oh, baby," she said, pressing my head to her belly.

"You think maybe I could get a handjob?"

She knows I'm not looking for pity. Or understanding. Or comfort. I'm looking for an orgasm—the only drug I have left. She doesn't just say yes. She issues a command.

"Get your butt up on the bed."

LISA IS EVERYTHING I am not—Irish, unself-conscious, quiet—and a few things that I am, most of them related to our mutual insanity. I was married when I met her to a potty-mouthed Cleveland girl whose mama was

---

Willie was twenty-three at the time; I was two. I'd say I've seen The Catch at least 500 times, and every time I see it I say the same three words: Fuck Willie Mays.

an A&P produce clerk, whose papa was a burger-flipper—married, monogamous, and loaded all day every day.

Living in Philadelphia, in 1993, I was working on a story about a local pedophile with AIDS who'd been popped after preying on two generations of Catholic high school boys, and one afternoon I saw Lisa—Elizabeth Riley Brennan—in the courtroom. A few days later we met for a beery lunch and fell at once into weed-fueled, slobbering *amour fou*. Heavy on the *fou*. She was thirty-six going on sixteen, limber as a Chinese gymnast, wild-eyed and wanton. She wore no makeup, had never even had her ears pierced, and her snatch smelled like a Moroccan bazaar. She set me on fire. She still does.

My wife never stood a chance, and I not only loved her, I had helped her get through med school. But by the time I sensed how far gone I was, I was too far gone to find my way back. Midlife-crisis heaven: Lisa covering the pedophile story for a newspaper in Philly, my wife working long hours at the hospital, and suddenly I'd found a wench who'd blaze, drink, and screw the night away.

The pedophile's lawyer handled my divorce. By that time, I was living in a one-room schoolhouse forty miles outside of Philly, with a tick-ridden mastiff and a shotgun and a special radio antenna to get broadcasts of the Indians games. A glossy men's magazine was paying me serious money to write juicy stories, and Lisa would come out on the weekends from Philly. We'd bang away on the air mattress—all the bedroom furniture I had—while Samson, the mastiff, stared sad-eyed, drooling.

• • •

THAT HANDJOB WAS, for me if not for Cleveland, the peak of the playoffs. I still believe that Cavaliers team was talented enough to win an NBA title. They'd run Orlando off the court in the first half game after game, and game after game the Magic's 3-point shooters would bring them back. Their coach, Stan Van Gundy, kept screaming that all they had to do was keep it close, that the Cavs couldn't handle pressure, and he was right. It wasn't just Mo Williams choking; it was the entire coaching staff, too busy with their clipboards to bother trying to light a fire.

By the time Game 6, and the Cavaliers season, ended, James was enraged—at Mo; at Anderson Varejao, who stopped fouling Dwight Howard despite James shouting at him to do so; at head coach Mike Brown, whose half-time adjustments seemed to consist solely of voiding his bladder—so angry that he stalked off the court without bothering to shake hands with the Magic.

James caught plenty of crap for that, but I loved it, and loved him for it. Orlando had focused its entire defense on him every game, and he had averaged an Oscar-like 38–8–8, arguably the greatest individual playoff performance the NBA has ever seen. That he refused to play the good sport in the aftermath of a loss was more than fine with me; after a lifetime of watching my teams take the

pipe, fuck sportsmanship. And screw the pundits who ex-
alt players as warrior-gods but morph into deacons at the
Church of John Wooden if an athlete dares betray a naked
human emotion that can't be crammed into a snickering
SportsCenter highlight.

That handjob and non-handshake were enough for me
to rise from the rocking chair and light out for the Lake Erie
shore. I'm from *Cleveland*, muffugga: I take solace and hope
wherever I find them. Championship or not, LeBron James
was the best basketball player I had ever seen. Dan Gilbert,
the Cavaliers' owner, would happily spend heavy to sign
the best available free agents. The star, the coach, and the
GM were all in the final year of their contracts. The entire
region—all of Ohio, in truth—would stand for nothing less
than a championship. Whatever was coming was sure to be
biblical. And I wanted to be there to see it, to bear—curse
you, Nike, and you, the Whore of Akron—witness.

Faith? An abstraction, nothing but cheap talk. Without
works, faith is utter bullshit; it even says so in the sequel to
the Torah. I would go forth to Cleveland, and live my faith.

I asked for blessing of my wife and son, my *Esquire*
boss, and my agent.

Only Lisa was particularly enthused, and I think it
was because her hand was getting chapped. I'm a man of
formidable appetite.

·   ·   ·

I LOVE NEW JERSEY, love my town, love the people. I love them because they remind me of Cleveland. I dreamed of becoming a sports columnist for the *Plain Dealer*, like the men I grew up reading: Hal Lebovitz, Bob August, Gordon Cobbledick. By the time I sobered up, I'd already overshot that mark; by the time I became a father, my favorite writer in Cleveland, John Hyduk, was paying his rent by loading trucks at a warehouse. I know now that I'm never coming back to Cleveland to live—and, knowing it, I love the place yet more.

It is not a simple love. My mother's here—Lucille Friedman Raab Mandel Michael—a woman I have tried so assiduously, and successfully, to avoid that she hasn't seen the inside of my house since Bush and Gore were fighting over who won Florida. If she has ever had a pleasant or lighthearted thought about anything having to do with me, she has never let a word of it escape her lips. My grandparents' old house is here, and sometimes when I come back I park across the street and wonder how I ever came out of it alive. All the scores I'll never settle, all the debts I can't repay, all my ghosts await me here.

And not only *my* ghosts. The whole place groans, sagging under fifty years of pain and rage. It is forever fourth down and 98 yards to go here, the Broncos' ball, with the Browns four minutes from their first Super Bowl; forever the ninth inning of Game 7, the Tribe leading by a run, three outs away from their first World Series win since

1948; forever the last second of Game 5 against the Bulls in 1989, with the Cavaliers up one and Michael Jordan with the ball.

Cleveland is each of those things plus a score or two more—the roaring silence that each failure has left frozen in its wake, here where hope and despair, love and hate, joy and sorrow, are inseparable. It is my favorite place on earth, the only home I'll ever truly have.

BY JUNE 25, less than a month after the loss to Orlando, I have a room at a Residence Inn a five-minute drive from the Cavs' practice facility, a $25 million, 50,000-square-foot, timber-and-stone temple of sport, built upon a rustic lot in the city of Independence, south of Cleveland. Dan Gilbert has built it here for one Babylonian reason: Independence is but a 10-minute drive from LeBron's 35,000-square-foot home—one complete with its own barber shop, bowling alley, casino, and a two-story, 2,240-square-foot closet—in Bath Township, close to Akron.

On June 25, LeBron is on vacation in Saint Tropez, wearing blue paisley shorts and a T-shirt that reads "CHECK MY TAT"; I am here in sweatpants and an XXXL Iron Man T-shirt because tonight is the NBA draft. And I am here this afternoon because of a press conference scheduled to officially announce this morning's news: Dan Gilbert has spent $21 million more to obtain the 50,000-square-foot, timber-and-stone temple of Shaquille O'Neal in a trade with the Phoenix Suns. Shaq, or what remains of him after 17 NBA seasons, is coming to Cleveland.

I don't know what O'Neal has left to offer the Cavs beyond his colossal ego and four championship rings, but that's plenty good enough for me. If nothing else, LeBron now has at least one teammate who has won big and won't tremble in the spotlight. If nothing else, the Cavs have dropped another cannonball into the NBA swimming pool. If nothing else, at least one Cleveland franchise has an owner willing to go balls-out every year.

But there is a problem, and he's now sitting at the podium about to begin the press conference: Danny Ferry, the general manager of the Cleveland Cavaliers, the world's only 6'10" midget.

His head is shaved—he started balding in his twenties; he's forty-three now—and his face is dainty, doll-like. Listed at 230 pounds in his glory, he looks thinner, slightly stooped, a bit stiff.

"It's been a busy week for everyone in the NBA," he says by way of opening. "We're all a little tired."

His voice is tentative, pitched high.

Opening question: "Did you run this by LeBron?"

"We talked to LeBron," says Danny. "We talked to a few of our players—we have an open level of communication with our team overall."

Oy.

Then: "How much was this move for LeBron's future beyond next season?"

"Obviously, LeBron's future is important to our organization," says Danny. "But this move and our goals are aligned with what our players want, including LeBron."

Gevalt. Two questions into this, two overarching truths revealed.

Truth 1: The Cavs are essentially owned by LeBron. The beat writers who cover the team clearly believe this—and they are a vastly more accurate gauge of reality than anything Ferry's likely to say.

Truth 2: Danny Ferry is so resentful of Truth 1 that he'd prefer not to acknowledge it.

Danny*ferry*danny*ferry*danny*ferry* runs locomotive through my brain. Danny Ferry came out of Duke and was the second player picked in the 1989 NBA draft, chosen by the Los Angeles Clippers. It was a historically bad draft, and the Clippers were a historically bad franchise. Danny Ferry, the son of an NBA lifer, left to play in Italy rather than sign with them.

The Cavs had a fine team then, a team so good that only Michael Jordan could derail them. But Cavs GM Wayne Embry, a good Christian gentleman who preferred to employ good Christian players, heard that Ron Harper, a wonderful young Cav who could score, rebound, pass, and defend, had been seen with nefarious people, in a nightclub of ill repute. There was even word of a "tray of drugs," media code for cocaine.

Harper told Embry none of that was true. He offered to take a drug test. But seven games into the next season, Embry traded Ron Harper to the Clippers for the rights to Danny Ferry. Embry even tossed in a couple of first-round draft choices, because Ferry was such a stud at Duke, not to mention a Catholic high school grad.

While Embry dickered with Ferry across the ocean, the Cavs won 42 games, missing the playoffs. Craig Ehlo filled in for Harper, which is why those 15 victories swirled down the crapper. Harp was only twenty-six years old. He played five seasons with the Clippers, ruined his knees, and still went on to win five NBA titles as a key backup with the Lakers and the Bulls. Ehlo won eternal life as the hapless yutz over whose pasty, upraised arm Michael Jordan launched The Shot.

Wayne Embry enjoyed a long, glorious career as an NBA player and as the league's first African-American GM, and it would seem unfair to judge him as a cretin based solely upon his having made the worst trade in professional sports' history, but it would not *be* unfair, however, because he also gave Ferry the dumbest contract in NBA history, a ten-year, $34-million deal, every year and penny of it guaranteed, thereby ensuring that Cavs fans would spend an entire decade watching Danny Ferry fail to live up to even a fraction of whatever talent Embry imagined he embodied. Too weak to bang with bigs down low, too slow to stay with any small forward, and saddled with a contract no sane GM would touch,

Ferry cemented Embry's idiocy for the 917 games that he played—a franchise record—almost always as a fixture on the Cavs' bench and as their best-paid and most loathed player.

Now, thanks to Dan Gilbert, who hired him away from San Antonio, Danny Ferry's back with the Cavs. El Jefe. Capo di Tutti Capi. Irony in khakis and a pair of boat shoes is now in charge, with complete contractual control of basketball operations, of finding a way to win it all, and win it all this year.

"Where is Shaq now?"

"I'm not sure," shrugs Danny Ferry. "I haven't spoken to him. His agent's in Vegas."

This is a man in charge of nothing.

IT'S LONELY ON the road. Even here. Especially here. If I come without my wife and son, I have no reason to see my mother. I'm long past the point of blaming her for my own *mishegas* or her own; she has been a little girl her whole life, and each of her three husbands and three sons has failed to deliver what she craves: a carefree life, preferably without end. If she saw me now—long white hair and beard, fatter than I've ever been before—the visit would last five minutes.

I have old friends here, too, but I have been gone so long, and have spent so many years alone inside my head,

trying to write, trying just to live a sane and stable life—
"Don't try," Bukowski said, but I don't want to die drunk
and full of aphoristic shite—I've grown more awkward in
the world even as I've made a place in it for myself, my
wife, my son.

And so I sit and read and think about LeBron. And his
mother. And her *mishegas.* She had no husband to divorce,
no parents' house to shelter her; she and her only son lived
a hand-to-mouth ghetto life. When trouble overwhelmed
her—and Gloria James has a rap sheet of her own for disorderly conduct and resisting arrest, and an affinity for
men who've done hard time—she found families willing
to take him in when need be, and she never let go of the
maternal thread.

Once it was plain that LeBron James was a hoops
Zeus—by ninth grade, the agents and shoe companies
were in full pursuit; after tenth grade, Michael Jordan flew
him to Chicago for a private workout—life and *mishegas* merged forever into a prolonged gold rush. While his
high school pocketed hundreds of thousands of dollars
by staging their games at the University of Akron's basketball arena, Gloria and LeBron tried to figure a way
for him to turn pro after eleventh grade. Her boyfriend,
who'd done a two-year stretch for drug trafficking, gave
the lad a Navigator and became his financial adviser. On a
subsequent birthday, Gloria negotiated a bank loan based
on James's future earnings and bought her Bron-Bron a
Hummer. The Ohio High School Athletic Association

cleared him on the Hummer but gigged him for accepting two throwback jerseys from a shop in Shaker Heights; after they suspended him for it, LeBron lawyered up and won a reversal.

It all panned out. The Cavs weren't the only NBA team that tanked games hoping to better their chances of getting James in the draft, just the luckiest. And even before the balls bounced Cleveland's way, Nike already had a deal with James that paid him $90 million.

I don't know that I'd trade Lucille for Gloria. Lucille had a taste for ex-cons, too—*aleva shalom*, Ray Schwartz, a gambling man who embezzled to make good his debt lest the loan shark kreak his legs—and a taste for the luxuries she'd never known. And I'm not entirely sure Lucille would swap me for LeBron. You'd probably have to throw in a second-rounder.

WHEN I HEAD back to the Cavs practice facility to watch the draft, Shaq's titanic head is filling the TV monitor in the press room.

"First, I wanted to send my condolences to the Jackson family," he says. "A legend has passed away today in the great Michael Jackson, so I want to send my condolences to his family."

What the *fuck*? Michael Jackson died? *Today*?

"I was elated about the trade," Shaq's saying as I grab

a spot among the real reporters, open my laptop, and hunt for online news reports, "because I get to play with one of the greatest players ever to play the game, LeBron James."

Yep, Michael's dead. Also Farrah Fawcett. And Yasmine. Sky Saxon—from the Seeds—too. Suddenly I'm not feeling too well myself. Big day for the Reaper. And the Cavs.

"I haven't had verbal conversations with LeBron," Shaq says. "But I've had many mental conversations with him. I know he's watching and I know he's listening right now."

Big laughs all around.

ESPN's rolling footage of young Shaq. With Penny. Then Kobe. And Dwyane Wade. Four rings.

"Remember," Stuart Scott is saying on the TV, "the city of Cleveland—not just the Cavaliers, the city of Cleveland—has not experienced a championship of any kind since 1964. It's been a long, long time."

That was the year that Michael first joined the Jackson Brothers. That was eight years before Shaq was born. That was—fuck it. This is the year all of that shit ends. Because Shaq is on the way. Shaq will foul Dwight Howard. *Hard*. He will drink deep from the fountain of youth. He will meld with young LeBron and make history. Together, they will redeem my ticket stub.

In the crowd shots from Madison Square Garden, where the draft is being held, Knicks fans are holding up LeBron jerseys in Knicks colors. Commissioner David Stern steps to the lectern.

"The thirtieth and final pick in the 2009 NBA draft, which the Cleveland Cavaliers have, and they select Christian Eyenga, from the Democratic Republic of the Congo."

The draft press guide is 200 pages thick; nowhere in it is anyone named Christian Eyenga.

"Eyenga," says Joe Gabriele, laughing. "Love that guy. That's the guy I targeted."

He's kidding. No one in the press room seems to have any clue who Christian Eyenga is. The Cavs media people promise a conference call with Eyenga. They bring out a DVD of Eyenga playing basketball in front of a crowd that seems to number about 18. He looks like a skinny high school kid.

Does he speak English? Yes, say the Cavs. But when the call is arranged, Eyenga speaks in French, to an interpreter.

He is pleased and proud to be drafted by the Cahv-va-yay, the translator informs us.

LeBron James is one of his idols. But whether the young man has had any mental conversations with Shaq, LeBron, or any other member of the Cavs organization is a question that goes unasked.

WITH THEIR SECOND-ROUND pick, the Cavs choose Danny Green, from the University of North Carolina, not to be confused with Irish Danny Greene, a legendary

Cleveland mobster. Green is a 6'6" shooting guard; Greene was the guy who helped Cleveland become the nation's car bomb capital in the 1970s. Green holds the UNC record for most games played; Greene holds the Cleveland record for most assassination attempts survived—he is semiofficially given credit for personally murdering eight Cosa Nostra hit men—until the day in October 1977, when he came out of his dentist's office and got into his car, whereupon a pair of nearby hitmen detonated the one parked next to his.

As soon as Danny Green's name is announced, Joe Gabriele says, "Shondor Birns is the only guy who can stop him." Joe remembers: Alex "Shondor" Birns was the last of a long line of Jewish gangsters in Cleveland, and Danny Greene's rabbi until they fell out over a loan arranged through the Gambino family, which eventually led to Shondor's untimely demise in 1975, when his Caddy exploded with Shondor inside of it, at least until the blast blew Shondor clean through his car's roof.

God almighty, it's great to be back home.

CHAPTER THREE

WITNESS

The day after the draft, I ate lunch with John Demjanjuk Jr., a Clevelander whose dad had been convicted of crimes against humanity and sentenced to die in Israel in 1988 for being Ivan the Terrible, an especially evil beast of a guard at Treblinka during the Holocaust. John Sr. had settled in Cleveland after the war, raised his family here, worked as a mechanic at a Ford plant in Brook Park, on the West Side of town, and became a local cause célèbre in the mid-'70s, when the Office of Special Investigations—the Nazi-hunting branch of the U.S. Department of Justice—put a bull's-eye on him.

The old man's deportation and prosecution took more than a decade, and it was always a huge local story in Cleveland, a city of ethnic enclaves divided into East and West by the Cuyahoga River. (Yep, *that* river—fuck you and Randy "Burn On" Newman very much.)

East dwelt Jews, Italians, and African Americans; the West Side was foreign territory full, in my imagination, of Eastern European goyim, like the Ukrainian Demjanjuks, and toothless white trash from West Virginia. East and West Siders didn't mix, save at ball games and at Cleveland State University, where I met Wife One. Her parents had never set foot on the East Side before the day of our wedding.

I'd wanted to write about Demjanjuk for twenty years. He had spent six yars awaiting execution in Jerusalem, until it came to the attention of Israel's Supreme Court that in fact a different Ukrainian had been Ivan the Terrible of Treblinka—never mind that a small parade of Holocaust survivors had sworn under oath that Demjanjuk was the very devil who'd strolled among the lines of naked Jews as they shuffled off to their doom, who with his sword had sliced the breasts off women, and whose bloody whip had forced young men and old to bugger each other while he watched.

It turned out—thanks mainly to years of investigative work by John Demjanjuk Jr. and his brother-in-law Ed Nishnic—that the same evidence that convinced the Supreme Court of Israel to set Demjanjuk free had been withheld from the Israelis by the Office of Special Investigations.

When Israel let John Sr. walk, he returned to Cleveland, and the OSI came after him again, accusing him this time of being one of the hundred or so Ukrainians employed by the Nazis as guards at another death camp, Sobibor. But they needed another nation willing to prosecute the case.

Israel? Fool me once. Ukraine? No sale. Poland, the site of Sobibor? Poland declined. But Germany was more than willing; you might even say the German agency equivalent to the OSI was eager for a show trial that would remind the world that the Nazis had ample non-German help when it came to exterminating Jewry. And so this *alte kocker*—John Sr., now nearing ninety—was again stripped of his American citizenship, deported to Deutschland, and charged as an accessory to the murder of precisely 27,900 Dutch Jews at Sobibor. Now I finally got a green light from *Esquire* to go ahead and do the story. It was an embarrassment of Cleveland riches—Demjanjuk *and* LeBron? If I peeked under my bed at the Residence Inn, would I also find Dennis Kucinich gift-wrapped there?

JOHN JR. SUGGESTED we meet at a restaurant called the Boneyard, more or less a sports bar with a pirate theme, including an exterior design featuring a phony-brick turret being climbed by effigies of human skeletons clad in shreds. It turned out to be a perfect place for an East Side Jew and the West Side son of an accused Nazi-death-camp guard to break bread. We talked about the Cavs, the Browns, and the Tribe. I didn't flash my Star of David tattoo, but John Jr., embittered by twenty-five years of media coverage that had presumed his father's guilt, was wise to me after I told him I'd grown up in Cleveland Heights—a Jewy haven.

I didn't give a shit about guilt or innocence—the judges in Munich would decide that—but I was looking for a measure of the truth, or as close as I could find after more than half a century. Good enough for John Jr. and Ed Nishnic, men of honor and integrity, Clevelanders. I figured when I was done reporting the Demjanjuk piece, I'd catch up with LeBron and the Cavs at training camp.

. . .

I'M PACKING FOR Munich when I catch wind of a story about a college sophomore dunking on LeBron at a skills camp James is hosting in Akron. The dunk itself isn't the news; the news is that some kid taped it and LeBron asked a Nike rep to grab the tape from the kid.

Damned if the Nike rep—his name is Lynn Merritt, Nike's director of basketball—doesn't walk up on the kid with the videocam, a Syracuse University journalism student named Ryan Miller, and tell him that filming the scrimmage broke the rules and so he'd better hand over the tape. Miller refuses, telling Merritt he was following all the rules. Merritt then speaks with a camp official who talks Miller into handing over his tape.

Dumb. But no big deal. Except LeBron insists he *didn't* tell Merritt to take the tape. Nike says Merritt wanted the tape because Miller broke the rules. But Miller, who comes off as entirely credible, says he checked with camp officials about the rules *before* he began taping; he says he was taping for hours prior to the dunk without anyone saying a word about it to him; he says that after he went up to LeBron to introduce himself, James then walked over to speak with Merritt, who then walked directly to Miller and told him to hand over the tape.

I'm reading Hannah Arendt and Gitta Sereny and Primo Levi, and now I'm thinking about LeBron James, the Chosen One—could he possibly be so insecure, so dumb, so egomaniacal, that he winds up making himself

into a total dickweed over a few seconds of video shot during an off-season scrimmage?

Yep.

I HURT MY BACK. I was Demjanjuk's son-in-law
following Ed Nishnic up the stairs to his apartment in
Cleveland and I stepped wrong, felt the twinge in my
lower back, and knew that within a couple of hours
I'd be locked into a week of constant spasm. It's part
of getting old, and part of being a fat fuck—and I do
mean *fat*: I've been a yo-yo for forty years, and at the
high end I'll bloat up past three bills easy—and nor-
mally I'd just take to bed for a few days, then resume
sitting and typing. This time, though, I fly to Munich,
drive around Germany with the lawyers and investi-
gators, fly to Warsaw and drive to Sobibor—near the
Ukraine border—then I drive back to Warsaw and fly
to Kiev, where I'd still be stuck in the mob at Passport
Control if a Polish pharmaceutical company executive
I met on that flight doesn't bribe my way past the lone
guard. Then I ride to John Sr.'s boyhood home, Dubovi
Makharyntsi, an off-the-map farming village of three
hundred or so Jew haters.

By this time, bouncing in the back of a Soviet-vintage
Lada shitbox over the rutted roads, I'm grunting with
each jolt, sciatic pain bolting down both legs. It's good, I

tell myself. I'm an addict living on a day-to-day reprieve. I don't use pain pills. I don't want to wake up two years later with another marriage destroyed and my son visiting me every other weekend or in jail. It's good, this pain. I'm here. I'm sober. I'm alive. Don't think about the pain. Think about the Jews.

Sobibor is a deeper, darker pain—an abyss of tribal hell carved into the dark woods, drenched in death. The disused train tracks ending just across from what had been the camp's front gate, the small wood house serving now as a rickety museum, the various memorials dotting the grounds. On a planet ruled by a species whose one universal language is suffering, some ghosts groan louder than others.

Still, you needn't be an anti-Semite or a self-hating Jew to be wary of the cheap and easy ways the Holocaust is used to remind all of the non-Jewish world of that which they're tired of being reminded of—especially by American Jews, especially when genocide has become unforgettably present long after *HaShoah*. I myself have come to resent—also to reject—all the endless, shrill *insisting*: that Jews be defined as victims; that Jewish history is but a parade of calamities; that Jews are God's chosen, which seems to me to underlie not only the Holocaust itself, but the very notion of it as a unique event to which humankind must pay eternal homage.

Good enough for me that my tribe itself survived. The fact that morons by the million cling to the belief that Jews have special, even demonic, power? Hell, that's just gravy.

Or maybe that's just me. I was moved profoundly as I visited the Wailing Wall in 1968, but when I wrote down my prayers on a scrap of paper and wadded and wedged it into a crack between the stones—as countless of pilgrims have done—I asked Yahweh to deliver unto my Browns a Super Bowl win, and unto my Indians a victorious World Series, and unto my harridan of a mother another husband, any husband, to get her off my back and get us the fuck out of the asylum that was her parents' house.

What I'm saying is that being a Jew and being a Cleveland fan are inextricably entwined to me. What I'm saying is that the saddest I feel on the Demjanjuk trip isn't at Sobibor; it's in my hotel room at the Warsaw Airport Marriott, when I go online and see that the Cleveland Indians have traded Victor Martinez to the Red Sox. I'm raising my son to be both a Jew and a Cleveland fan because my sense of duty—practical and spiritual—trumps my fear that in so doing I am inflicting needless suffering upon the innocent whose soul I treasure most in all the world. Martinez, who signed with the Tribe when he was sixteen and wept in the clubhouse when he met with the media after the trade was announced, is my son's favorite player, and my own—and now he's one more name to add to the list of our favorites who'd left the team and its fans behind. Victor is a wonderful ballplayer, a switch-hitting catcher, a rare talent; now he is gone. One more T-shirt that my son, *kinehora*, will soon outgrow, another bobble-head over the fireplace, gathering dust.

So Martinez cries while cleaning out his locker in Cleveland, headed for the Red Sox; I cry in my hotel room in Warsaw when I see the clip. My fists are clenched. If my back wasn't locked into one elephantine knot I would throw myself onto the bed. Or order a huge room service meal. Or both.

No doubt, I'm insane. If the crux of ardent fanhood holds a touch or more of madness, then Cleveland fanhood is a bug-eyed, shit-smeared lunatic, howling for a God who's never going to come.

But I saw Him once, I swear. I even saved my stub.

ANYONE WITH ANY experience around alcoholics and other drug addicts will tell you that when it comes to long-term sobriety, bet on the substance, not the addict. Because when you stop using the drug, you're the same scared, sorry-ass bastard who hid for so long—who threw life away rather than face living without being baked beyond sentience all day every day. Some folks can abuse any kind of drug and stop when the pain grows too great to bear; alcoholics and addicts never stop, because they're too numb or frightened to feel the pain. They *get* stopped—by the law, by the intervention of friends or family, by the hand of fate or the angel of death.

How's that sound? It sounds to me like a fucking addict, which is what I am, talking shit with another fucking addict, which is exactly what I'm doing. Because I have one last job to do before the Cavs assemble at training camp: a cover story starring my favorite former crackhead, Robert Downey Jr.

We're in Pacific Palisades at his rented house, just after Labor Day. Cavs Media Day is three weeks off, the Demjanjuk story's done and I'm only home for two days—just long enough to pry open Downey's febrile brain and think about visiting my old man.

THE COOK SERVES LUNCH. Microbrewed root beer. Steak salad. Gluten-free cake. My back is killing me—I rode to the gate at Newark airport in a wheelchair—but I'm here and it's all good, brother. Hanging here now, listening to Downey's patter, and the birdsong, feeling the breeze—call me a hack, call me a starfucker, but today, the only voice in my head is the gruff yet tender farmer's: This will do, pig.

Downey's about to release *Sherlock Holmes*—the first one—hence the cover. I'm trying to pry something out of him about Mel Gibson, who's in trouble again.

"He'll be okay," Downey says. That's all Downey's going to say. I know that. I respect that. I met Downey in 2005, just before he started shooting *Iron Man*, and we got to know each other a little bit. But Mel Gibson's his friend. And I'm a magazine writer.

His father sure didn't do him any favors, I say, speaking of Mel's Holocaust-denying lunatic of a sire.

"Whose has?" says Downey.

Not mine.

"You're not even going to drop by this time."

Nope. He's banging a Gypsy. She's into him for three grand so far.

"What's his name?"

Sanford. Sandy. Long story.

"No, no. *No!*" Downey shouts. "I want it. Dude, I'm not fucking around."

His own father, a filmmaker, was getting Downey high before he turned ten. Out in the distance, a few miles past the Getty Center, Sanford Raab is mourning his recently deceased second wife in the same way he honored her in life, by having sex with some floozy—in this case, a Romani bimbo who hit on him in a supermarket parking lot—who'll steal every cent she can.

The key here, the through line for these fathers and their sons, is simple but hard to accept, especially for a star of the silver screen: being an alcoholic and an addict—trying and failing repeatedly to stay sober, going off to rehab or to jail—bespeaks a certain panache and offers a showcase for drama, especially out here. Being mentally ill, though, is nothing but a buzzkill. It's unsexy. And it's not conducive to steady employment, in or out of the performing arts. Yet if you scratch most high-functioning addicts, you'll find a self-medicating soul tortured by an exquisite pain your standard-issue street-sleeping drunk can't afford to indulge.

The last thing Robert Downey Jr. or Mel Gibson or my father—with no savings and no income beyond his Social Security check to pay for his cigars and Viagra—is going to publicly admit to is suffering from a bipolar disorder. Me, I'll confess to anything short of killing Tupac.

He's in love, I tell Downey. Told me that he hasn't been this happy in years and years.

"Everyone's happier after they get worked by a Gypsy," Downey says.

Who *doesn't* love a Gypsy? Besides Hitler, I mean.

"It would be fascistic to hate Gypsies."

After lunch, we're going to Venice, where Downey and his wife have just bought a place. I can barely walk; yesterday, I tell Downey, a gate agent saw me crooked with sciatica, and called in a wheelchair. Pushed past all the glaring assholes in the security lines, I couldn't help smiling.

"I'm so sorry your back is fucked up," Downey says. "But can I say—and I mean this in the most nonfascistic way—that's a true Gypsy move, dude, the wheelchair thing."

Downey tells me his chiropractor is stopping by the new place in Venice—an entire building, four floors of mahogany and metal topped with a rooftop pool—at eight p.m. If I hang out, he'll ask the chiro to do whatever it takes to get me upright for my flight back home in the morning.

Which is how I wind up on the phone—the chiropractor's cell—with Shaq. Hollywood magic: The chiropractor, Dennis Colinello, works on Shaq's back, too, and so when I tell him I'm writing a book about the Cavs, he phones Shaq's service, leaves his name and number, and a few minutes later—I'm on a massage table at Downey's, and Colinello, a big, beefy fellow who brings tremendous gusto to his job, has fingers of steel clamped upon a bulging disk low on the left side of my back, squeezing it away from the nerve—Shaq calls back and Colinello hands me the phone.

Couldn't be more psyched, I tell Shaq, trying not to yelp as Colinello works me over. Lifelong fan. Ticket stub. LeBron. 1964.

"All right," Shaq says. His voice is deep and quiet, a cavern of repose. I'm squeaking like Mickey Mouse. LeBron. Starved fans. Orlando. Kid holds down the fort. Now, you. Four rings. Fucking cavalry.

"All right."

Seriously, man. The missing piece. You.

"All right."

See you at camp, Shaq. Look forward to shaking your hand.

"All right."

Every word I squeak at him I believe. He's old, yes; in NBA terms, he's ancient. But he rolled into Cleveland for a press conference the week after the draft, and unfolded a photo of Danny Ferry and O'Neal himself, an inelegant action shot showing Ferry bending over to grab a loose ball with Shaq's groin pressed hard to Ferry's ass. Shaq referred to Ferry as "the great Danny Ferry" a couple of times, and informed the Cavs head coach, Mike Brown—sitting on Shaq's other side—that the team would not be double-teaming the opposing center anymore. He proclaimed himself the dun dada of NBA centers, vowed to win a ring for the king, all that shit—and every boast was music to me. Four rings. Four fucking rings.

THREE WEEKS LATER, on September 28, I'm back at the Residence Inn for Media Day. They put a nice board under the bed for me and my back. There's a Chipotle nearby, and a Zoup!, and a Bob Evans. I'm not sure what food group sausage gravy belongs to. I am sure that I don't give a fuck.

The first and last words Shaq says to me when I get to the practice facility and shake his hand are "Santa Claus." The belly and long white beard and hair. My hand grasped by his disappears completely, like my son's in mine.

LeBron is leaning against a wall, behind a semicircle of reporters and cameramen four and five deep. He says he looks forward to playing with Shaq. It's humbling, he says, to play with an all-time great. Says his free agency options are open, but his sole focus is on winning a title. Says he's still not sorry he didn't shake hands with the Magic. No, he's not worried that Shaq will clog the lane and make it tougher for him to slash to the basket.

He looks bored. Every answer is rote. He gives the appearance of human engagement—his eyes widen, his brow knits—but never does he come close to cracking a genuine smile—or nod hello to one of the handful of beat reporters who've covered him for six years and more. Vacant.

I don't know what I was expecting, but I've profiled pro athletes for twenty years and more without ever sensing disengagement so profound. The kid is twenty-four; he seems twice that age today.

"LeBron does what LeBron wants to do," Joe Gabriele tells me when I sidle over to ask him about it.

What does he want to do?

"Nothing."

Gabriele writes a column for the Cavs website. "The Optimist," a title drenched in an irony enriched by those decades of defeat, but also a tribute to how utterly James has transformed the franchise.

You ever get a sit-down with LeBron, Joe?

"Nope."

Never?

"Nope."

How come?

All Joe does is shrug.

Everyone but LeBron seems to be in a pretty good mood.

Mike Brown, the Cavs head coach, young, pear-shaped, and sunny, is fairly glowing with good cheer.

"LeBron has accepted me with open arms," he says. "Every time I've asked him to do something, he's done it."

Lordy. You'd never guess from this kind of mealy-mouthed, aw-shucks stuff—"LeBron allows me to coach him," he says in answer to another question—that Brown is now in his fifth season as head coach of the team; he talks like the video assistant he once was. I know the NBA is a player's league; maybe Phil Jackson once said the same thing about Michael Jordan, but it's hard to imagine Jackson sounding so earnest and grateful about it. Brown sounds like he's still on probation, maybe because he is.

Delonte West, too, seems to be in fine spirits, particularly for a young man with bipolar disorder who was pinched by police not long ago while riding his three-wheeler armed with three loaded guns, including a shotgun stashed in a guitar case strapped across his back. Not such a big deal, he tells reporters. He's taking his meds now. Feeling good. I want to believe him—West is a yellow-skinned, ginger-haired sly-boots with darting eyes, a scruffy goatee, and neck tattoos, half gangster, half stoner—but he literally can't stand still.

Mo Williams seems lost in the shuffle, a small man among titans, dapper even in sweats, with a trim mustache. No one asks him about his shooting against the Magic. Mo has tweeted over the summer that he'll do better next time—and after all, this isn't New York City, where the *Daily News* or *Post* surely would have run a back-page headline during the Orlando debacle screaming "SCHMO WILLIAMS" in 96-point block capital letters. Here in Cleveland, especially on Media Day, nobody wants to rock this boat, this team, this last best hope—this year—for a championship.

INCLUDING ME. The first time I go to meet with Dan Gilbert, owner of the Cavs, he's at the team's executive offices on the sixth floor of the Q. The LeBron Christ banner rules the view from the floor-to-ceiling windows, high above the Cuyahoga. If he can get a statewide issue passed, Gilbert wants to put a casino on the shore. A house afire, Dan Gilbert. *Intense* is far too mild a word: this Yid once got into a fistfight at a friend's son's bar mitzvah. My kind of guy.

I tell Dan flat out: I can't score a bucket, shoot a free throw, grab a rebound, or set a pick; I can't help the Cavaliers win a single game in any way that doesn't involve a sniper rifle and a life sentence; I'm going to write a book about the upcoming Cavs season come what may, but I've rooted for Cleveland teams with all my heart for all my life, and I'd rather see the Cavaliers win the NBA Championship than write a bestseller.

We're in a big conference room, just me and Dan and my ticket stub, which I now remove from the Ziploc bag and slide across the table to him. He picks it up and studies it for minute, turning it over in his hands. Gilbert is not a large man, but he's a power lifter, a no-necked, thick-chested, thin-lipped brick of a billionaire, a Detroit guy who builds business after business after business, beginning when he was an undergrad at Michigan State, running football pools.

"This is great," Gilbert says, looking at the ticket. "You were there?"

I was there. I was twelve years old. I've been waiting my whole life for another one. I'm counting on *this* team to do it *this* year. You hold on to that stub for me, Dan—for luck.

Gilbert smiles. "I'd be afraid to lose it," he says, pushing it back across the table. "But don't worry. We'll get you one to go with it."

I'm looking past him, out the big windows. We're on the sixth floor, and I can see in the middle distance the crooked river winding out of the old smokestacks of the Flats—where they milled steel around the clock, once upon a time; where blue-collar guys whose wives stayed home to raise the kids put those kids through college on those wages once upon a time; once upon a time, right here in Cleveland, there lived a middle class—and into the trees of the valley beyond.

I'm looking past him and I'm thinking about what that day might feel like, after the Cavs win the NBA crown, and how completely unprepared Cleveland fans would be to deal with that kind of joy. Yeah, it's only sports, asshole. Cleveland Heights City Hall is a car dealership, the 9th Street Pier and Captain Frank's Lobster House is the useless motherfucking Rock and Roll Hall of Fame, the old Arena—the Cavs' first home—is a rubble-filled lot, and the stadium where the Browns beat the Colts in 1964 was torn down so that a new football palace could be placed directly upon its burial ground. It's only sports.

I'm not sure what Cleveland fans will do when their next champions are crowned, but I don't think they'll be setting cars on fire and breaking windows. I think they'll walk out of their homes and head downtown, to Public Square, gather in drunken clumps, some howling, some praying, and hug it out till daybreak. I believe that Cleveland will never be the same; it will be a better, happier place. I truly believe that Cleveland's collective soul will be redeemed on that great and glorious day. Nothing less.

I'm crying again—sitting across from Gilbert, who says, "It's all right," when I squeeze out an apology for my lack of decorum. "It's fine. I understand. Believe me. I get it."

A ridiculous business, sports. Pathetic, no? I couldn't have imagined as a twelve-year-old living in my grandparents' house that someday I'd be a husband and father and writer, that I would be sitting here in this man's office, blowing my nose and wiping my eyes because—of all the things in the world to care about deeply—I care so much about Cleveland and these doomy fucking teams.

"Let me ask you something," Gilbert says. "That banner"—Jesus James—"don't you think it would be better if it said, 'We Are All *Witness*' instead of 'witnesses'?"

It's Nike's banner, not Gilbert's, and I suppose it would

work just as well with "witness," and I tell him so. Either way. But I'm thinking about how long and at what depth Gilbert must have pondered this issue while slowly going mad.

Is he going to stay?

Gilbert shrugs. "Nobody knows. I think he will. I'm counting on the fact that out of all the guys he's surrounded himself with, he's the smartest one by far. I took him out to Sun Valley in July"—Sun Valley, Idaho, hosts an annual three-day retreat for the most powerful moguls in America—"and I saw guys pushing Warren Buffett and Bill Gates out of the way so they could get close to LeBron. He's young but he's from here, and he knows that's a part of what makes him so special. I read about how he's influenced by people around him, but I've gotten to know him and he's going to make up his own mind."

He needs a championship, I say. Now. This year.

"And he'll get it," Gilbert says.

I'm worried about Mike Brown. I'm tired of hearing him say how honored he is to coach LeBron.

Gilbert winces. "I don't like hearing that either," he says.

I don't know if any coach has ever been under more pressure to win it all. Or any GM, for that matter. You've got Danny Ferry in the last year of his deal. No extension. Now or never.

"We're all in," Gilbert says. "All of us. All in."

CHAPTER FOUR

THE KING'S
HUMANITY

*W*e have no choice but to go to war with the dick we have—to live our lives forward, despite knowing, like every Cleveland fan, how it's all going to end. Death's certainty is a fact, which is perhaps why humankind—even Jews—clings to the irrational: to laughter, love, and the faith that existence will end well, which is to say that it will never, ever truly end.

I never believed that Cleveland or its teams were cursed. Truth is, I came to believe that the Cavs were going to win it all—and that LeBron would re-sign with the Cavs—until the season ended. The fan's heart holds fast to hope. And, even after hope is fled, to memory.

There may be a parallel earth in a parallel universe, a dimension of being where The Shot rims out, The Drive falls short, Jose Mesa closes out the ninth inning of Game 7 in the '97 World Series, LeBron and the Cavaliers win an NBA Championship, and I sport six-pack abs and a nine-inch cock—but I sure as shit can't see it from where I'm sitting.

IT'S A RAINY Saturday in early October, three weeks before the 2009–10 season starts, the day of the annual Wine and Gold scrimmage, part of the polyamorous marriage between LeBron and the Cavaliers and Akron and Cleveland.

It didn't begin with LeBron James, that marriage. For

twenty years, the Cavs' home was the Coliseum at Richfield, a 20,000-seat, $36 million precast concrete palace plunked into the nowhere of greensward halfway between Cleveland and Akron in 1974. The idea was that five million folks already lived within an hour's drive, and that the two cities someday would form one megalopolis—and so slick Nick Mileti, who owned the Cavs plus a pro hockey team, put up the Coliseum, complete with luxury suites, unheard-of at the time, and a two-floor penthouse apartment for himself. Nick even convinced Sinatra to open the joint before all the asphalt was poured in the parking lots—and, yeah, the whole megalopolis thing turned out to be a silly vision, but it was cool at the time, and it gave all the Rubber City yokels a chance to see their teams without risking their soft asses on the hard streets of Cleveland.

The Cavs moved back downtown in 1995. The Coliseum was demolished in '99. Legend has it that the wrecking ball bounced harmlessly off its poured-concrete skin on the first pass. But after drafting James, the team began holding a preseason intrasquad game at the University of Akron's basketball arena, known locally as the JAR, so named for one James A. Rhodes, the pinhead governor who ordered the Ohio National Guard to Kent State University—a few miles away—where they proceeded to gun down four students on May 4, 1970.

It's barely noon and the JAR is packed already—5,500 fans here to see an intrasquad scrimmage. They know the way: this is where LeBron's high school moved its home games when they realized how much more money than a bake sale could be siphoned from his growing fame.

I'm heading down the hall to the Cavs' locker room when Gloria James blows by—I can smell the fumes trailing in her wake. Wine. Red wine. No visible gold.

She's a small woman clearly accustomed to a crowd parting as she barrels toward it—not unlike her boy. She looks *younger* than LeBron, actually; she's wearing too-tight jeans with back pockets filigreed in shiny silver. His brow is plowed with deep furrows; hers is baby smooth.

Gloria smiles a feral, bloodshot smile at a Cavs PR person, rasps, "Tell my son I'll be out there," and motors on down the concourse.

Her temper is lore among the local media; none of the beat guys ever come nearer to her than a nod. They say she kicked out the back window of a police cruiser once, after being pulled over for driving under the influence. During a playoff game in 2008, Gloria went after Paul Pierce when Pierce pulled LeBron out of bounds. Kevin Garnett kept her off Pierce with an arm around her shoulder. When LeBron—still tangled up with Pierce—saw her, he yelled, "*Sit your ass down!*" Gloria didn't blink. She just went on as she was pulled away, still "motherfucking" Pierce for messing with her boy.

HER SON HAS Akron's area code, 330, tattooed on his right forearm. These 5,500 people are up on their feet just because he's out on the court; he has made his team and its fans feel like family. Before he joins the layup line, James comes over to the stands to kiss the two young boys recently adopted by teammate Zydrunas Ilgauskas and his wife from Z's native Lithuania. Then Anderson Varejao, the Cavs power forward, walks up to press row to shake hands with the writers, smiling like a young Brazilian with a new $60 million contract. The guy is gorgeous: a valentine of a face, a head full of bobbing corkscrewed curls, 6'11", an altar boy's sweet smile.

Seems like a happy young man, I say to one of the beat writers.

"He should be. They replace thirty percent of the dancers every off-season just to keep him fed."

Shaq, he draws the loudest cheer. He looks heavy. Looks old. Slow. Who gives a shit? He's *Shaq*. He's *here*. He'll play himself into shape.

Nobody breaks a sweat. It's a party, a picnic. LeBron's squad gets whipped, Shaq's wins: the big man scores 12 points without once lifting both feet off the floor. Everyone's happy. Hell, even *I'm* happy, and I can barely walk for the pain in my back and legs. So many Cleveland fans so high on a fucking scrimmage. It was no dream: both LeBron James *and* Shaquille O'Neal. Who's good enough to stop these Cavaliers—hungry, playoff-tested, and armed now not only with the best basketball player in the NBA, but with this living giant fighting by his side—who will keep them from the Grail? It may be raining in Akron, but for a Cavs fan there's not a cloud in the sky.

EXCEPT DELONTE. A few days after the Wine and Gold scrimmage, before a preseason game, one of the beat writers mistakes a nod from Delonte for an actual greeting and asks the kid how he's doing.

"Step the fuck off," West snarls. "Motherfucking faggot. *Fuck* you."

The media relations folks hustle the press out of the locker room. Delonte dresses for the game but never takes the floor. The Cavs announce that he's excused from practice for a few days—personal reasons. And nobody in the media says or writes a word about his locker room blowup except for one blogger, who takes down his post after a phone call from the Cavs insisting that the incident had never taken place.

Poor Delonte. There are the pending gun charges from his preseason arrest, of course, and a short-lived wreck of a marriage, but underneath all that is a sweet, funny young man from DC with severe bipolar disorder, off his meds and out of his fucking mind.

West himself had gone public about his mental illness the season before, when he took a leave of absence from the team. This time around, he's in no shape to talk— word is, he's holed up in his Cleveland condo, suicidal—

but the men in charge of West's professional life, Danny Ferry and Mike Brown, act like none of this is of any pressing interest, and the media seem just fine with that.

"I haven't spoken with Delonte," Mike Brown tells the media pack after another practice without West.

This strikes me as odd. As he walks back to his office, I ask Brown why he hasn't talked to Delonte himself.

"Danny's handling it."

But you're his coach. Is there a problem between you two? Aren't you worried about him?

Brown looks pained but says nothing. Ferry says nothing. The media say nothing. LeBron says what a teammate needs to say—that West is a brother, part of the family, and that the Cavs will be there for him when he's ready to return—and that's that.

FINE: IT'S MENTAL ILLNESS, not as easy to discuss as a broken wrist. Fine: the focus must stay fixed upon the team's mission. Fine: I'll reluctantly admit that the beat writers who justify avoiding the subject may really be acting out of respect for Delonte's privacy and concern for his well-being.

But as the season unfolds, Delonte West starts to seem like a keyhole, a way of seeing into an organization operating in extremis. He was my favorite Cav last season, the anti-Mo—a skinny 6'4" dervish, quick enough to lock down opponents on D, fluid enough on offense to create his own shots, and fucking *tireless*. He played more playoff minutes than James himself, and never seemed overmatched by the moment.

West finds his way back to the court during the first week of the season, but he never gets his job back as a starter—and he never speaks a word in earshot of the media. He sits alone in front of his locker before and after every game, staring into space, silent. Not once do I hear his voice or see anything resembling an expression on his face. No teammate ever speaks to him during the period reporters are allowed in the locker room. Postgame music blaring, players howling with laughter, the media pack going back and forth from LeBron's corner double-wide to Shaq's locker next to West's, and Delonte, oblivious to all of it, sits there, eyeless, earless, voiceless. And no one ever writes or speaks of this, as if mere mention of his shade—the shadow of Delonte West—is understood by all to be taboo.

I ask Shaq about him one day after practice.

"I don't know what that word *bipolar* means," he says, "but basketball-wise, I want him in there. If I'm going to war, I'm taking him with me—two minutes left, I want him in the game with me. He's got that dog in him."

The dog?

"He got the *dog* in him, definitely."

I see the dog on court once in a while: Delonte faking a pass and flashing like a blade to the basket; cutting back on defense at the very moment an opposing guard tries to push the ball through a lane suddenly owned by West. His hustle at those times bespeaks his swagger; unlike LeBron, he never beats his chest, never flexes, never howls.

More often, though, West just looks dazed out there. A few times, he goes quietly berserk, hissing profanely even as he dribbles, and Mike Brown calls time-out and pulls him from the game. Delonte walks to the end of the bench, finds an empty seat to slump into, and drapes a towel over his head.

ALL THAT TRULY matters, mind you, is that the Cavs win and win and win. I study Delonte because he is bipolar—I am haunted by the same ghost, and by my memory of Tony Horton, a Cleveland Indian who broke down during the 1970 season and tried to kill himself, then quit the game forever at the age of twenty-six. I had booed Horton unmercifully and at great length that same summer, when I myself was eighteen and batshit crazy, goofy enough to have snuck inside the Stadium on Banner Day with a huge "HORTON STINKS" sign—but when the Cavs take the court, when the lights go down and 20,562 Cleveland fans, their pockets full of money, their hearts full of hope, their lungs of leather filled by lust for victory, bellow as a single cry of hunger after a half century of famine, then the blood of communal passion washes me clean of every fanatic sin, and leaves me trembling.

It could not be so without LeBron James. Alpha dog. Omega Man. Moses. Christ. Our fucking savior. He sits unmoving as the other starters are introduced—his right leg crossed upon his left knee—and the flames belch from the JumboTron and the spotlights swing toward him, and finally he rises, and as he does, the voice of Cleveland rises with him, until the unblinking Cyclopean eye of the sports cosmos—otherwise known as ESPN—turns to fix itself at last upon Cleveland, Ohio.

Not once a season: the world watches every time he takes the floor. Across the universe, he is belovedly *LeBron*—and has my poor hometown ever before boasted a one-namer, a star of such magnitude as to be known by all of sentient humankind merely by his or her first name?

Harvey? *Who?* Pekar. *Who?*

Drew? *Who?* Carey. *Get the fuck outa here.*

Arsenio? *What?* Hall. *What?*

Maybe Satchel, for a brief moment, in the United States of Baseball. But Satch was no native son.

Jesse Owens, greatest of all homegrown Cleveland athletes, ran Hitler's faith in Aryan supremacy into the ground at the Berlin Olympics in 1936, winning four Golds. "Cleveland" was Jesse's middle name, for fuck's sake, but he was born in Oakville, Alabama, and didn't move to Cleveland till he was nine. Besides, even in Cleveland, Paige and Owens had long ago vanished into history. LeBron James was *making* history, game by game, unfurling it across the firmament.

The Cavs sat me in the upper reaches of press row, between two young men typing stories about LeBron James in Chinese. We look at each other sometimes after a LeBron slam or chase-down block, and let our mouths fall open and widen our eyes in tribute to his force. We never speak a word, nor need to—we have found an international way of saying *What. The. Fuck.*

The Lakers come to town in late January and the Cavs whup them up and down the floor—LeBron has 37 points while Kobe shoots 12–31, and Shaq and Varejao reduce Gasol and Bynum to a stiff pudding—and after the game I waddle through winter's mist across to East 4th Street, an alley when I was young, now a half block of upscale food joints. I limp into Lola, order the beef-cheek pierogi and a hanger steak, and feel better about Cleveland than I have since boyhood. People living in suburbs flung far from downtown—on both sides of the Cuyahoga River—now drive into the city to see the Cavs and get a bite to eat. They are loud, happy, proud to be part of a city many of them left behind decades ago.

They are no longer from Rocky River or Solon or Avon Lake or Chagrin Falls; every last mother's son of them is proud to be from Cleveland, motherfucker. *Cleveland.*

. . . .

ON THE COURT, the Cavs flow, or don't, through James. There are games, and lengthy stretches almost *every* game, where the offense boils down to LeBron, possession after possession, pounding the ball at the top of the key, looking for a cutter or an opening to drive, while the rest of the team stands in place, watching the shot-clock wind down, all of them—Vladimir, Estragon, Pozzo, and Shaq—waiting for LeBron.

Off the court, LeBron also leads a team. The Cavs employ his cousin and personal assistant, Randy Mims, officially in some security capacity; in reality, Mims is James's Minister of Ritual Handshakes. Maverick Carter, LeBron's cousin, friend, and longtime business manager—like Mims, Carter's an Akron guy—is a fixture at the Q and comes to practice when he feels like it. Lynn Merritt, LeBron's Nike guy, is omnipresent. Gloria, Queen Mother, strides the bowels of the Q before and after games like she owns the joint.

What I never see is Mike Brown or Danny Ferry speaking to LeBron. Just before the All Star break, one beat writer asks Brown if he has any problem with LeBron entering the dunk contest; LeBron's doing his annual will-I/won't-I dance about taking part.

"I don't get a vote," Brown says. "I don't get a vote in anything."

If he means it as a joke, someone needs to tell his face.

. . .

"MY GAME WON'T let me score a lot of points," LeBron says one night in November after another Cavs win. He's at his locker, facing a larger crowd of media people than usual; the Knicks are visiting, and the New York City papers all have at least one writer in Cleveland for the game, including a *Times* freelancer who's been hanging out trying to do a story about James's obsessive pregame rituals. Day after day after day he awaits his brief audience with the King, and day after day after day the Cavs' media relations folks shrug and shake their heads.

"My game won't let me score a lot of points": it sounds odd in and of itself. Plenty of athletes refer to themselves by their first names, including James, but LeBron alone has ascribed a separate existence, complete with volition, to his array of skills.

Odd, too: tonight LeBron has scored 31 points by early in the second quarter, and finishes with 47. What he seems to be explaining is why he didn't go off for 80 or 100 points, which, in view of the Knicks' lack of ability and interest on defense, might have been well within his reach.

"If I'm doubled, I pass," says King James.

The writers stand, impassive. LeBron weeks ago stopped taking questions about free agency, after Dwyane Wade was quoted as saying he talked to LeBron about joining forces and reporters begin pressing James about it. But the New York guys, their audience back home certain that James and his Yankees cap will never spurn a chance to play in New York City, still come, hoping to squeeze blood from a stone as their editors hope to squeeze blood out of them.

"LeBron, how much do you know about Walt Wesley?" one of the writers asks.

"Who?"

"He's the guy whose record you broke for points in a half?"

"What's his name?"

"Walt Wesley."

"Not a lot. When he play at?"

In my mind's eye, Wesley's still playing. He was the best player on the first Cavs team, a 6'11" center. I see him even now, another ghost; from my $1 student seat in the old Cleveland Arena on Euclid Avenue, I can hear him, too—"*Hee*-yur, *hee*-yur," he cries out to his guards from the low post, begging them to find some way to pass the ball to him. Forty years and a sea of Stroh's ago, and Walt Wesley is still planted in the lane—his ass thrust back into the other team's big, his gangly arms reaching forward to catch a bounce pass that never comes.

"Thanks, guys," LeBron says, his nightly sign-off.

"I'm bored past the point of caring," says one of the New York writers. "I don't think anybody gives a shit anymore. Get the fuck to July 1. I've got nothing left to say about LeBron and 2010 and the Knicks and the Nets and the whole fucking thing. I'm done."

. . .

I DON'T THINK much about LeBron leaving. All they have to do is win, and everything else will take care of itself. I stand with Joe Gabriele watching practice the day before the Magic visit in February, and I point at the few sad banners hung high on the wall—a conference championship, a couple of division titles—and shake my head.

Nothing to write home about, I say.

"That's about to change," Joe says. "You can feel it."

I feel it. Orlando comes and the Cavs whip them good. LeBron has 32 points with 13 assists, Delonte has one of his best games of the season, and Shaq bangs Dwight Howard to a draw. The next day for lunch I take my cousin Jeff to Slyman's, and we fall upon corned beef sandwiches moist and fat, mounds of salt meat stacked on soft rye, the single greatest deli sandwich in all creation. I order two more for the seven-hour ride back home, and scarf them both by the time I get to Niles—sixty miles—where I have to find a bed, and sleep away my Cleveland gluttony.

MY PLAN TO break through the wall between LeBron and the media is simple: I'll profile Shaq for *Esquire*. I can't pitch a LeBron profile, because *Esquire* just ran a story about him a couple of years ago. I didn't write it—a woman did, and Maverick Carter tried to fuck her. But Shaq hasn't been profiled by anyone for years, and surely LeBron will give me five minutes.

No dice.

"LeBron likes to do things in volume," the media relations chief tells me after two weeks of waiting. "In other words, he'll take several pending things that he's got to do, and instead of spreading them out to keep it light on any particular day, he'll do nothing on several days, and all of a sudden he'll say, 'I'm going to do all of this tomorrow.'"

Jesus. Now I *know* I'm fucked: I'm not going to get a single second with LeBron. I'm facing a tall wall of bullshit without anything resembling a gate.

So I wait until the media scrum breaks up after the next Cavs game and I sidle over and ask him what Shaq has brought to the Cavs.

"What's he brought to *me*?" LeBron says. He looks shocked, even a bit resentful, as if I am implying that King James somehow may have been missing something. Or maybe he's only surprised to see Santa still hanging out at his locker.

"You know," I stammer. "The four rings, the big personality."

"Ahhh, I'm the same," says LeBron. "No matter what teammate come upon this team, I'm going to be the same guy."

I stand there, staring at him, waiting.

"I love my teammates. I respect that."

Still waiting. Best tool in journalism: waiting.

"But the fact that—when you have Shaq, it's a different commodity. It's a different guy."

Waiting.

"He's a four-time champion. Everybody knows what he's been able to do on the court, but off the court—he's much better off the court than he is on the court."

Huh? It doesn't sound like he's criticizing Shaq's on-court demeanor or play. In fact, Shaq has played himself into shape—for the first time, he's willing to appear before the throng of media in the locker room without a shirt on—and with him playing well, the Cavs certainly look like the best team in the East. The chemistry between Shaq and LeBron on the court seems fine, although there are times when Shaq feels LeBron isn't going to the basket often enough.

"If we're in a game and he misses four or five jumpers," Shaq had told me, "I don't want to see my guy miss that many shots, so I'll just tell him, 'Drive.' I always tell him, 'Drive.'"

I'm about to try to push LeBron in that direction myself—and maybe jam something in about the book—when he smiles. He seems less tense. He is shifting into full bullshit mode.

"We're kind of similar, honestly. We're both like big kids that love to play the game of basketball—have fun every single day, do a lot of laughing, do a lot of joking.

And the fact that we are the same—it's easy for us to get along."

He turns to finish getting dressed. I walk away, straight into the towel receptacle, a large wooden open-topped bin on wheels, waist high for normal folk. I stagger on the thick carpet, but manage to right myself without falling. And as I gather myself, I catch a sideways glimpse—here I'm going to flout what is unarguably sports journalism's most precious and closely guarded rule—just a snapshot, really, of the Chosen Junk.

Eh—nothing special. Proportional, which is to say larger than my own cock last time I managed to find it.

I TAKE ONE last shot at James, in Newark, in early March. Shaq tore a ligament in his right thumb against the Celtics a few days ago and just had surgery in Baltimore. He isn't with the team, and I figure this might be a good time to sidle up to LeBron again. Sooner or later, damn it, we're going to bond.

I wait for the media scrum to clear out, but the Cavs' media relations folk have other plans. They usher a local TV reporter and her cameraman past me, and in spite of her tight skirt and high heels she somehow manages to lower herself onto the floor in front of King James, who seems absolutely delighted to make her acquaintance.

"I'm trying to figure out a way to ask you the question without you getting mad at me," she says.

"Oh, I don't get mad," says LeBron. "I've heard the question over and over, so at this point we just gon' see what happens. It's a long ways away—we'll see what happens. I'm very happy with what's going on in Cleveland. I've given everything to this franchise and they've given everything back, so . . ."

I go looking for the head of media relations to ask him if it might help my cause to hire a hooker.

CHAPTER FIVE

COINS ON
A COLD GRAVE

eing Jewish and being a Cleveland sports fan have always felt to me like the same thing. I see little material difference between "Wait till next year" and "Next year in Jerusalem"—both are variations on what might be called the Dayenu Principle, which exists in a spiritual realm where both celebration and sorrow meld into a single chord that first fires the heart, engorges it with hope and joy, then bursts it apart in icy agony.

"Dayenu" is itself the theme song of the Exodus, a Passover tribute to God's power and goodness, and also a Hebrew word whose meaning is "It would have been enough for us." Pesach is unarguably the peak of our tribal history, above even the Great Koufax's refusal to pitch a World Series game on Yom Kippur. The song is more than a thousand years old, 15 stanzas in praise of Yahweh. On and on and on it goes: To deliver us from bondage? Enough. To split the sea and drown our enemies? Enough, enough. To give us the Commandments and the Torah and the Sabbath, to deliver us unto the Holy Land—ENOUGH!

Dayenu is an endless paean exalting a God who has chosen the Jews as his people. Applied to Cleveland sports, on the other hand, the Dayenu Principle pays tribute to another Power beyond human ken, whose ineffable puissance buttresses a single tenet: suffering is inescapable.

To lose and lose and lose again is never loss enough.

Time after time, with each Cleveland team, I have whispered "Dayenu" to myself, bitterly, and felt that mystery of God trembling in the air, foul as rotted flesh. But only as the Cavs' season winds down do I begin to grasp the full cruelty of its existence.

I am, as ever, first met with hope. The Cavs play a faster, more fluid offense with Shaq out, and do just fine. They clinch the best record in the league early enough to let Mike Brown rest LeBron for the final 4 regular-season games, casting their gaze to Chicago in the opening round. Shaq has rehabbed his thumb, dropped 15 pounds, and shaved his beard; he looks 10 years younger and raring to go. The city is geared up for another run at the NBA championship, hoping that this time—this time—next year will finally arrive.

DAYENU.

It was bad enough, in the waning moments of the first round's final game against the Bulls, for us to witness LeBron James shooting a free throw left-handed. Bad enough, for us to be told—*after* that free throw—that he had played with an injury to his right elbow for weeks; bad enough, that the precise nature of his injury existed in that ethereal realm beyond even the vocabulary of the Cleveland Clinic's best doctors.

Bad enough, to hear LeBron proclaim, "Cleveland fans don't have any reason to panic," before the Eastern Conference Semifinals against the Celtics, as if Cleveland fans actually needed a reason to panic.

The Cavs open slow in Game 1 at the Q against Boston, then blow the Celtics off the hardwood. LeBron finishes with 35 points, 7 boards, and 7 assists.

Panic? Us? No fucking way. We got you, babe.

NBA commissioner David Stern hands James the MVP trophy at center court before Game 2, and James raises it high to each corner of the Q. I've got tears in my eyes up in Section 130's press area—to hear that prideful roar, to see all those fans up on their feet, to watch a Cleveland player accept an MVP award: I've never before seen the like of it.

And then the whistle blows—Dayenu—and LeBron wobbles through Game 2 as if hungover. He scores 3 points in the first quarter, 5 in the second, and 4 in the decisive third, when the Celtics pound the Cavs 31–12. The Cavs lose, 104–86.

Dayenu? Fuck, no.

Bad enough, to see LeBron outplayed by the ghost of Rasheed fucking Wallace.

Bad enough, to see Mo Williams shoot 1–9 and serve as a human traffic cone for Rajon Rondo, who had 19 assists.

Bad enough, to watch Shaq rendered null on both ends of the court by Kendrick Perkins, to watch Delonte wander the court like a wino in search of his cardboard box, to see Mike Brown's vaunted defense shredded for 83 points in three quarters.

Bad enough, to see Brown fuming at his postgame press conference, so mad that he even unleashes a "God damn"—the first time all season I've heard the coach swear—only to be followed to the podium by an insouciant LeBron, who shrugs off a reporter's question about Brown's anger.

"Maybe he talks that way to you guys," quoth he. "I didn't hear none of that. I know we have to play with more urgency. The series is 1–1. There's no panic for me. I've been in these situations before."

Indeed, James has. But—Dayenu—the Cavs have lost each and every time.

AND *AGAIN* WITH the panic bullshit? Nobody else is talking about panic except for this too blithe young gent whose team has just played like shit in a playoff game against an older, smarter bunch of veterans who two seasons ago won it all. The Cavs have just blown their home-court advantage in a lopsided loss to the most storied, successful franchise in league history—and excuse me, pal, but you played like crap.

And the elbow—the streets are filled with a dull muttering that James's Game 2 fog was due to an injection to soothe his pain.

"I don't want to use the elbow as an excuse," he says, a phrasing perfectly equivalent to using the elbow as an excuse.

It gets worse. Over the two-day break before the series resumed, I hear from multiple sources that the Cavs were partying on the evening before Game 2, after LeBron's personal MVP ceremony at the University of Akron, and had greeted the dawn in a state of groggy disrepair. Not a mere handful of players, mind you: more or less the entire team. They played like they were hungover because they were.

GAME 3 IS A MIRACLE—deliverance from doubt, our hope restored, our faith affirmed. LeBron hits for 37—he alone outscores Boston in the first quarter, 21–17—and the Cavs hand the Celtics their worst home-court playoff defeat in all their fabled history. As the final horn sounds, the Boston crowd boos its aging champions off the court.

Two days later and again LeBron and the Cavs come undone. In Game 4, James has the same number of turn-overs as made baskets—7—while Rondo puts up 29 points, with 13 assists and an amazing 18 rebounds, a testament to both his own gifts and the Cavaliers' bizarre passivity.

It is a 10-point loss that looks and feels like 50. Shaq,

who played better than any other Cav, refuses comment after the game; he is furious with Brown for not putting him back into the game late in the fourth quarter when Cleveland mounted a doomed comeback. Brown clearly lost the thread tonight; never a strong in-game coach, he rotated players off the bench seemingly on a whim. It reminds me of the Orlando series last season—Brown has more options now, but no more of a clue.

The same goes for the team. The Cavs played tonight's game as if their Game 3 rout of the Celtics had been a knockout punch, like they felt Boston would go down easy. Now the series is heading back to Cleveland tied 2–2, and the Celtics look not only like the better team, but also far more resilient and determined.

In Game 5—Dayenu—James does something he has never done before: he chokes. Shut out—*scoreless*—in the first quarter, he attempts only 4 shots in the entire first half and finishes with 15 points on 3–14 shooting for the game.

The Cavs lose, 120–88. In the most important game in franchise history, the two-time MVP plays the worst game of his career.

Dayenu?

Absolutely not. No way. Not nearly bad enough without LeBron's postgame presser.

"I put a lot of pressure on myself to be the best player on the court," he says. His cream T-shirt matches his sweater perfectly and his golden earrings and wristwatch sparkle in the TV lights. "When I'm not, I feel bad for myself—because I'm not going out there and doing the things I know I can do. I spoil a lot of people with my play. When you have three bad games in a seven-year career, it's easy to point that out."

Enough? Too much. Too much, to ask LeBron to carry a team, and too much to ask him to satisfy the yearning for redemption of millions, and too much—way too much—to ask him to comport himself with any measure of grace or grit in the wake of abject failure.

Bad enough? Fucking ridiculous. Our warrior: a feckless child stunted by a narcissism so ingrained that he's devoid of the capacity to respond to failure with even a semblance of manhood. The *fans* are spoiled? In King James's playhouse, there are no mirrors.

"As far as worried about the series," he added, "I'm not worried about it."

Meanwhile, the Cavs have lost two home games by a total of 50 points to a team they were heavily favored to beat and are on the verge of a final meltdown.

Thank God, though, nobody seems to be panicking.

TURNS OUT THAT LeBron truly isn't worried about the series.

It ends against the Celtics, in Boston, in Game 6. LeBron puts up an empty triple-double, plus a ghastly 9 turnovers.

It ends with a minute and a half to go in their season and the Cavaliers down by 9, with their head coach on his feet, windmilling his arms, urging them to foul, begging them to push the ball upcourt, pleading with them to keep trying.

The Cavs prefer not to. They won't foul. And when they get the ball, they simply let the clock run out. Not happy to lose, but perfectly content to stop trying to win. They quit.

Quit on their coach and on each other, quit on their fans and the city that loved them.

And then their leader, LeBron James, the camera tracking in front of him on his way through the tunnel to the locker room, tears the jersey off his chest and tosses it away. As if he has gone down fighting. As if he gives a rat's ass. As if every basketball fan watching—and every basketball player—hasn't just now witnessed the truth revealed.

LeBron James is a fraud. No guts, no heart, no soul.

DAYENU?

Don't be silly.

"I'm not using the elbow as an excuse," LeBron says after the game. "It limited me some."

A reporter kindly points out that the elbow might've limited him plenty. "It seemed like there was a large part of your game missing," says the reporter.

"Well, I got a lot of time to think about it now," LeBron says.

Odd: he keeps right on talking, answering a question that hasn't yet been asked.

"I have no plans at this point. I've made no plans. Me and my team"—his other team, the Akron chapter of Mensa—"we have a game plan that we're going to execute, and we'll see where we'll be at."

Then comes the inevitable follow-up question, about free agency.

"I love the city of Cleveland, of course. The city, the fans. It was a disappointing season, to say the least. But at the same time, we had a great time together. We'll see what happens."

Dayfuckingenu. Cab fare's on the dresser, bitch. Close the door hard behind you. The lock sticks.

THE RUMORS ABOUT Delonte West and Gloria James start filling my e-mail in-box almost as soon as Game 6 ends. There are several versions, but each begins by referring to a source—a mortgage broker, a general contractor—who has done business with the Cavs, and goes on to assert that LeBron found out that West and Gloria James were sexually involved, and that the Cavs' playoff trail of tears may be traced to his discovery.

In walking back the rumor with folks close to the team, one source tells me that there was a loud argument in the locker room before that game, during the course of which Delonte screamed, "I'm gonna fuck yo' momma," at LeBron.

I don't buy it, and I can't find anyone in a position of genuine knowledge who does. I think Gloria James ill-used her son in some obvious ways from the instant she gleaned how many hundreds of millions of dollars he might be worth, but I have no doubt at all that she loves him fiercely, as he loves her. To suggest that she betrayed their bond by consorting with a teammate says more about the rumormongers than anyone else.

Truth is, not even the Dayenu Principle covers this sort of thing. The most salient and sane explanation I can find for the best player in the NBA having three of the worst games of his career in one playoff series on the verge of his free agency has nothing to do with sex, and it comes from a source I consider both impartial and unimpeachable: despite his frequent postseason brilliance, James has always had problems coping with playoff stress. Through his last few seasons, he has suffered—come the games that matter—a range of unreported maladies, including shingles, back spasms, and chronic indigestion, and it has been a source of ongoing concern for the Cavaliers. But perhaps not for much longer.

. . .

MY FAVORITE STORY of Cleveland fanhood is about an old friend of mine named Joey, the 1997 World Series, and a shortstop who played for the Indians nearly a century ago, Ray Chapman. Chapman was a fine ballplayer and a sweetheart of a guy, much loved by his teammates; he batted second on one of the greatest Tribe teams of all, the 1920 Cleveland Indians.

Those Indians won the World Series—1920 and 1948: that's the complete list in 110 years—but Ray Chapman wasn't with them. He was hit by a pitch in a game at Yankee Stadium on August 16, 1920, and died early the next morning.

They brought his body back to Cleveland and buried it in Lake View Cemetery, one of the world's greatest boneyards. I shit you not: Lake View holds more than 100,000 former people, sits on 285 gorgeous acres, and is the resting place of James Garfield; Eliot Ness; John D. Rockefeller; Carl Stokes, the first black mayor of a major American city; and the ashes of the finest writer Cleveland has ever produced, Harvey Pekar. It always was one of my favorite places to get high and—far, far less often—laid.

Ray Chapman's grave is hard to find. The granite monument that marks it—paid for back in the day by donations from fans—simply bears his full name, Raymond Johnson Chapman, along with the years of his birth and his death, 1891–1920. Joey had never visited, but he figured it couldn't hurt to pay homage in the fall of '97 before the Tribe took the field down in Florida to play the deciding game against the Marlins.

He found the grave in an old section of Lake View, near the Euclid Avenue gate, spotted it standing by itself amid a row of unraised markers. As he walked toward it, he saw something else: the top of Chapman's headstone was covered end to end with the coins of the Cleveland fans who'd already made the same Game 7 pilgrimage.

The story ends, naturally, with Jose fucking Mesa blowing his third save of the Series in the ninth inning. It ends with the Tribe losing, 3–2, in the eleventh, on an unearned run after an error by Tony "Feh" Fernandez on a routine ground ball to second base. It ended for me in the rocking chair in North Jersey—with Lisa trying to console me. I told her the same thing I always tell her in those moments: I'm good. I'm used to this shit from a long way back. I'll wake up tomorrow morning with you next to me, a job I love, cash in my wallet, and money in the bank. You want to feel sorry for somebody? Feel for those poor fucks in Cleveland who were ready to head downtown and revel for the first time in their lives in the only joy strong and wide enough to bridge—to *transcend*—50 years of collective civic misery.

RAY CHAPMAN WAS twenty-nine when he died. He was a jug-eared kid from Beaver Dam, Kentucky, who still kept his United Mine Workers card in his wallet after eight seasons in the majors. In *The Pitch That Killed*, one of the greatest baseball books ever written, Mike Sowell notes that when Chapman's salary was bumped up to $3,500, Ray bought himself silk shirts and handmade suits. Pro baseball was a business then, too, far uglier in crucial ways than today—the year before Chapman died, the Black Sox had thrown the World Series. But for a poor boy born into a hardscrabble, hand-to-mouth existence, making a living by playing the game had to feel like nothing short of a miracle.

LeBron James was born into blight on the west side of Akron, and the fact that the world of professional sports had been transformed into a carnival of global scope by the time he came along hardly negates the astonishing nature of his flight to riches and glory. It happens to poor boys in other sports and from other tribes; once upon a time, Jews dominated pro boxing and basketball in America.

James did not choose to be born in Akron, and he did not choose to play for the Cavs when he entered the NBA. The team tanked shamefully during the season to improve its draft position, chose him, and that was that. It never was clear that LeBron wanted to play for Cleveland in the first place, and he made plain—in word and deed—his desire to maximize his future options when his rookie contract expired and he chose to sign a three-year deal rather than four, or five, or six.

Looking back . . . fuck. *Fuck.* Listen: I don't want to

return to Ray Chapman's era. I believe in free will, free lunch, and free agency. I believe I can offer no more than an educated guess at what's in my long-fingered wife's heart, or my sweet young son's—or, frankly, my dog's. Too many days even now, pushing toward sixty, I remain a stranger to myself.

What then can I read upon the stone heart of LeBron? What can I learn from the odyssey of a black kid, sprung from the loins of a teen mama, fatherless save for the seed of himself, who was a rock star at the age of fifteen, with girls lining up to lay naked with him just so that years later they could boast to their boyfriends that they had boffed King James?

That he's an asshole? I knew he was an asshole years before he became a free agent. The whining and ref baiting; the tough-guy scowling and biceps flexing belied in every instance by his failure to step up for a cheap-shotted teammate; his ludicrous sideline dancing in the fourth quarter of Cavs' routs: he is a hideously poor sportsman and more adept each season at acting every inch the prima donna bitch.

But despite all of that—*and* the Yankees cap at Jacobs Field, *and* the refusal to commit to a longer contract that would've relieved some of the win-now pressure on the front office, *and* the disillusioning up-close view of an entire organization warped to fit his whims—despite it all, he is still my asshole.

Our asshole.

I never loved Lake Erie any less when it stank of piscine death. I didn't have Chief Wahoo tattooed on my left arm in tribute to Albert Belle's integrity and Manny's mental hygiene. And I didn't have to like the Whore of Akron just to love him. His game, great as it was, was only part of our intoxication. Because he was one of us, a landsman, son of the same soil, a member of the tribe.

None of this makes LeBron's performance against the Celtics—not only his play, but also his comportment—easier to explain or excuse. Quite the opposite: for fans whose bond to the spirit of Cleveland sports is a legacy dating back a century, bequeathed by a father and grandfather, it was a betrayal most profound. It was stupid and selfish enough to call attention to his elbow; had he not shot the free throw left-handed in the Bulls game, nobody outside of the team itself would have known about what was a minor injury. It was beyond stupidity and selfishness to tell the fans that they had been spoiled by his excellence. It wasn't only Clevelanders who watched LeBron James choke and quit. He brought disgrace and dishonor upon the city, and that went far past the game: it went straight to the heart and soul—*his* heart, *his* soul.

And yet, and yet, and yet, and yet. The same fans famished by decades of defeat, still so full of hope and hunger that they paid homage by the hundreds at the grave of a ballplayer few of their fathers had been alive to see play: Who among us hopes LeBron will walk away from the Cleveland Cavaliers?

• • •

THE CATCH. The Drive. The Fumble. The Shot.

Dayenu: The Decision.

Coming to a cable channel near you.

July 8, 2010.

Too late for Cousin Jeff: Season-ticket holders had to renew and pay for their seats long before the free-agency period began on July 1.

Too late for Mike Brown, too. Gilbert fires him despite Danny Ferry's objections, and when Gilbert makes plain that he, not Ferry, will choose Brown's successor—that, in fact, the owner wants more of a say-so in running his team—Ferry resigns. He is replaced by his lieutenant Chris Grant, who has never been a GM before, but who also holds the distinct advantage of *not* being Danny Ferry—not the $30 million albatross that hung for a decade from the Cavaliers' neck, not the benighted Dookie who spent five years and hundreds of millions of dollars more failing to win a championship with the NBA's best player.

Surely by the time Ferry decides to quit, he already has seen LeBron's Larry King interview, featuring the following slip of the tongue and semi-revelation:

"The team I go to, or whatever the case may be, will have an opportunity to win championships in multiple years and not just because of LeBron James," James tells King.

Old and worn as Larry is, he's still sharp enough to catch the tell, the giveaway: "*The team I go to . . .*"

So Larry does what Larry has done since the days when Major Bowes had a radio talent show: he lobs LeBron a softball—"Does Cleveland have an edge?"—and James says, "Absolutely. Because this city, these fans, have given me a lot in these seven years. For me, it's comfortable. I've got a lot of memories here, but it's going to be a very interesting summer and I'm looking forward to it."

Golly. Thanks for the pig ear, you worthless mother-fucker.

James has cut off all direct contact with the Cavs. Won't even take Dan Gilbert's calls. Three weeks ago, the Cavs were up 2–1 against the Celtics. *Three* fucking *weeks*. Now the Cavs have no coach, a rookie GM, and no firm reason to believe that LeBron James will ever play another game in a Cavs uniform.

Bad enough? You've got to be kidding. Dan Gilbert goes rushing after Tom Izzo, the coach at Michigan State, Gilbert's alma mater—a man with no NBA experience at all. Izzo bites down hard—who wouldn't, for $6 million per annum?—but he'd like a word with LeBron before he officially takes the job. Nope. Which, when you ponder it—James is unwilling even to speak with the man the Cavs owner is hoping will become the team's coach—is eloquent beyond words, a fuck-you as clear and direct as any prospective head coach, and any franchise, could hope to hear from any athlete.

Izzo decides that he's better off preaching defense and loyalty to teenagers who might not have realized that their coach was on the brink of breaching a deal at MSU that ran until 2016—and so Gilbert signs Byron Scott. Scott has coached two New Jersey Nets teams to the Finals—they lost both—and won three championship rings from his playing days with the Showtime Lakers.

It's a brilliant hire, truly. Scott was a big part, along with Magic and Kareem, of those Lakers teams coached by Pat Riley, and he won his rings playing for his hometown fans. He's tough, he's confident, and he's all grown up. He's willing to take the Cavs job without any assurance that LeBron will stay.

A genius move, absolutely perfect in every way save the only way that now matters: it comes a year too late, or two. For had Byron Scott coached the Cavs against Orlando in 2009 or Boston this season, the Cavs—and LeBron in particular—would've had a battle-tested leader on the sideline, in the locker room, and in their faces, to steady and support them and, if need be, back them down. Scott's three rings with the Lakers confer all the NBA gravitas, and command all the NBA respect that Mike Brown's clipboard and Danny Ferry's Duke degree do not.

Scott drops by LeBron's skills camp in Akron a few days before The Decision. He stays an hour or so. No, he tells the media the next day, he didn't speak with LeBron.

Untrue.

Scott saw James and said, "Hey, LeBron."

LeBron said, "Hey, Coach."

Nothing more?

"Nope," says Scott.

Seems strange.

"I didn't go there to woo him."

No. Of course not.

WHEN I LEFT Cleveland in 1984—I'd finished, at the age of thirty-one, a B.A. at Cleveland State University, the Harvard of Euclid Avenue, and got into the University of Iowa's Writers' Workshop—I always figured I'd be back. I'd spent a year or so in Los Angeles in the early 1970s, three years in Austin in the late '70s, and always I came back to Cleveland to live. When my first wife got into medical school in Iowa after my two years at the workshop, and then into the University of Pennsylvania for her residency, I still thought of Cleveland as home, still came back for the Tribe's last series at the Stadium, for Opening Day at Jacobs Field, and for Cavs playoff games, and to watch the Indians in the World Series. Before my son, God love him, ever set foot in Yankee or Shea stadium, I took him to Cleveland to watch his first major-league baseball games.

My first feature for GQ—assigned in 1991 by the editor who's still my boss today—was the story of Kevin

Mackey, the Cleveland State basketball coach who had a wife and children in Shaker Heights and a double life as an inner-city crackhead. Over and over I wrote about Cleveland and Clevelanders, and I'd go back to the city, find a room in a downtown hotel with a view of the lake, and sleep like a baby in the womb. Nobody in the city knew who I was, knew or gave a shit what I was writing or what I had written, and that was fine by me. The places I wanted most in all the world to see—the ruins of League Park, where Speaker, Ruth, and Chapman played; the art museum lagoon, where I once had pledged my love to a girl by throwing my first handgun into the muck; the softball field behind my junior high school, where I had jacked a drive to right-center field that cleared the tall fence and landed on the tennis courts beyond—all were there.

I didn't come to see people. I avoided everyone, including my mother. People wanted things from me. Cleveland *gave*. It wasn't nostalgia; it was plasma. It was who I was. Here was the diner where I sat over a plate of runny eggs after finally—*finally*—getting laid. Here was where I brought a tumbler of Jack Daniel's to my Classics in Translation final exam and, when I realized I couldn't write a fucking word in the blue book, bargained with the professor for that semester's C. Here was where I walked into drugstores with forged prescriptions and walked out with a hundred quaaludes. Here was where I left the shoe store where I worked with the day's deposit and a stolen credit card, headed for the airport, and caught a flight to London. Here was where I walked in on some asshole who'd broken into my place to steal the drugs I was dealing and tore an ear half off his head.

ON THE MORNING of July 8 I get a call from Joe Gabriele.

"Don't worry," Joe says. "He's staying."

You *know* that? Don't fuck with me, Joe.

"I'm just saying. You know how when he gets fouled hard he goes down and acts like he's hurt? This is the same thing—he's got everyone right where he wants them, thinking they know what he's going to do. He's going to fool them all. He's staying."

I don't believe it. I don't even believe that Joe believes it. The reporters closest to James and Maverick Carter, Chris Broussard and Stephen A. Smith, say it's going to be Miami. I believe them. And by now—I've been blogging LeBron's free-agency countdown on Esquire.com and Deadspin—I'm too numb to hope, almost past caring. Almost? Never.

When showtime rolls around, I'm in the rocker. Lisa's on the couch. My son is over on Douglas Street, playing group tag—"Manhunt" they call it. I'm well pleased with the boy, *kinehora*. I don't want him sitting here on a summer night, watching this nonsense, don't want him to see the old man sickened and enraged one more time by my love for Cleveland sports.

When I see the footage of LeBron with the little boys and girls, I am both sickened and enraged. Idi Amin: I'm watching LeBron James, the last king of Cleveland, using children as props, as ornaments, as moral deodorant.

You want to stay, whore, stay. You want to go, whore, go. But spare us an hour of ESPN eunuchs lapping your scrotum while you void your bowels and bladder on the only fans who'll ever love you like a member of the tribe.

Or do you need this charade? Is it fun and exciting?

Nice shirt, asshole. Nice neck beard.

Wow, I'm so ancient I remember Jim Gray before he was a sock puppet waving a "Will Fluff for Food" sign.

South Beach? When did the Heat move to South Beach?

What a grotesque and bloated parody of a man you turned out to be. Nothing but a bum. That's the mot juste: bum.

I WATCH EVERY MINUTE. Every second. I'm sorry it doesn't go on longer. I want to hear this narcissistic asshole refer to himself in the third person a few more times. I want to hear him calling himself a "twenty-five-year-old man" again, too. I want to hear more about the dream he had this morning, and about talking to his mama; hey, if he goes for another hour or two, he might even mention, at least once, Savannah Brinson—his high school sweetheart and his sons' mother.

I also want another hour of live shots from Cleveland, especially the two squad cars parked, lights flashing, beneath the Banner, bulwarks against the pillaging horde. Someone needs to get on the radio and tell them that the horde left a long time ago, took its talents to the suburbs and beyond, and took with it all the disposable income and every vestige of hope.

"I'm sorry," Lisa says when it finally ends. "That was horrible."

So strange. I know this feeling in my bones—Cleveland lost—but there was no game. And this, this is worse. What the hell are they going to do? Gilbert isn't going to stay in Cleveland if the team starts losing money every year. The Browns are clueless. The Indians have lost their way, along with most of their fans. What's the city going to do if it starts losing teams?

"You want a handjob?" she asks.

Eh. I'm really not in the mood. I have to post something about this train wreck tomorrow, and I have to think about what to think before I can write.

"Why don't you just get your butt up on the bed?"

Yes, ma'am. God forbid that I should be the first man in human history to say no to a handjob.

· · ·

I SEE A prima facie case that James contrived years ago to join Dwyane Wade and Chris Bosh in 2010. They entered the NBA at the same time, became teammates and pals playing for Team USA in 2006, and each signed a three-year contract extension in 2007 that would enable them to become free agents together.

I also give James credit for being savvy enough to keep that option open.

Savvy is as savvy does. I discern the thumbprint of a cabal—not the tinhorn Rubber City rube posse led by Maverick Carter, but the Creative Arts Agency, whose client list includes James, Bosh, and Wade—yet the fact is, LeBron James at age fifteen betrayed his own Akron community by going to a predominantly white Catholic high school rather than playing for Buchtel, a public school populated mainly by African Americans. It was a hugely controversial, carefully calculated move, and an early warning that his notion of loyalty was fluid rather than fixed, and utterly self-serving.

Likewise, I can argue that the Miami Heat, in the persons of Pat Riley and Dwyane Wade, are guilty of tampering, of illegal contact with James before he entered free agency, but the fact is, no major move goes down in the NBA's flesh bazaar without back-channel negotiations. That's part and parcel of the meat-peddling milieu enveloping ballers far less blessed than LeBron James as soon as they're old enough to help an AAU shaman build his stable of pimpable talent. That's what enables leeches like William "World Wide Wes" Wesley to act the playa. At any level, amateur or pro, prizefighting is a less dishonest sport.

I'll take all of the above and, above all, this: LeBron James is no naif, no victim, nobody's fool but his own. Same with Dan Gilbert, me, and every Cleveland fan above the age of consent who believed that what James said counted more than what he did. For years, James let folks far and wide know that he would be available when he became available. He saw teams strip themselves of talent for two seasons to gain enough payroll space to woo him. He bade them parade to Cleveland in their suits, while he wore shorts and a T-shirt to the meetings where they trotted out their PowerPoint charts and pleaded for his favor. James didn't *make* them beg; he *let* them.

And no other franchise or city groveled like poor Cleveland and the Cavaliers; none had so much to lose. The Cavs put people at key overpasses and downtown street corners to hold signs printed with "Mission" and "Community" and "Family" in hope of catching the King's eye as he passed on his way from Bath Township to his free-agent pitches in downtown Cleveland. A "We Are the World"–type video featured the governor of Ohio, while the Cleveland Orchestra played a free concert on Public Square in the heart of downtown on the evening of July 1 with fireworks, a special musical tribute to James, and the word "HOME" spelled out in lights on the office tower across the way.

Dan Gilbert put half a million dollars into his pitch. There was a heart-wrenching video filled with plain folks—black and white, old and young—just talking about what James meant to them and to Cleveland. And there was a cartoon video full of fart jokes and lampoonery, wherein Pat Riley, stripped to a Speedo and gleaming with baby oil, invited LeBron to strip down and wrestle.

In the end, Riley needed no videos. Riley brought what money can't buy—a bag full of his championship rings, in silver, in gold, in platinum—shoved it across the table to LeBron, and said, "Hey, try one on."

THE CATCH. The Drive. The Fumble. The Shot. The Decision. One of these things does not belong. One of these things was an evil man's willful act, and worse. The Whore of Akron knows full well he has stomped on Cleveland's soul.

He doesn't care. To care, he would need a soul of his own—a soul and a sense of good and evil. The Lubavitcher Rebbe, no hoops fan, defines evil as good's absence. The Decision: evil. Not pure—nothing human ever is pure—but evil nonetheless.

Just sports? Fine, so it's not war, or plague, or famine. But evil doesn't get a pass just because it hasn't literally murdered the innocent.

I am ready to give up, to write off the season past as a

romp in sports journalism fantasy camp. I've seen enough: enough defeat, enough behind-the-curtain ugliness, enough civic suffering. I can't help the Cavs or Cleveland or myself. So I won't live to see another champion; so I'll die a froth-mouthed fan: So what? Enough. Dayenu.

Then, inside me, something shakes awake. Overnight.

It is not merely Dan Gilbert's letter to Cavs fans, a Comic Sans yowl of betrayal, mingling scorn, curse, and random syntax to near-Wagnerian effect.

It is not merely the Heat's welcome party for the Big 3, an event that resembles nothing so much as Saturday night at the Crazy Horse, with Stormy, Windy, and Princess each riding her own pole.

It is not merely the communal lap dance that follows, with the Whore of Akron telling the Miami mob that winning will be so easy that Pat Riley can suit up and play point guard, that he, King James, has come to deliver championship after championship—not four, not five, not six, not seven—on and on until his braggartry is washed under by the roar of a sea of sun-baked cretins who fancy themselves fans.

It is all these things, and it is more than all these things; my debt to Cleveland and to all who suffer as I suffer has come due.

What the hell. I'm taking my talents to South Beach, too.

CHAPTER SIX

CHIEF WAHOO
AND
THE WHORE
OF AKRON

ear midnight, the plane circles over the Atlantic on its final descent and I see one moon fat in the black-blue sky and another shining up from the dark water. The city skyline shimmers, dotted with light. Gorgeous, all of it.

I haven't seen Miami in ten years. On the ride from the airport, the early autumn air is thick and soupy; downtown rises on the horizon, so white, so glittering, so clean. It is a world apart from Cleveland. Or New Jersey.

Tomorrow is Media Day for the Heat. I've got an hour with Dwyane Wade beforehand for an *Esquire* fashion spread. This took weeks to negotiate—the team is in full lock-down mode, and the media relations people have alerted Wade's publicist that I'm writing a book.

And not just a book. "We are aware that Scott is writing an unauthorized book about LeBron James, so any questions about him is completely off-limits," is how the publicist put it in an e-mail to my editor. I'm unsure which tickles me more, the subject-verb problem or the "unauthorized." I've spent the entire summer trying to convince the NBA office that since I've been a journalist for twenty-plus years for major national magazines, and since I have a book deal with a respected publisher, I might be worthy of the same credential the league grants to the yobbos who duct-tape ESPN's power cords to the arena floor.

No dice. Why? The reasons change. There is some mention of a policy, but no actual policy. The man in charge takes umbrage when I suggest that the whole process seems dishonest. His name is Tim Frank, and he is a senior vice president of the NBA. I know—surely Tim must also know—my request is nothing illegitimate. But The Decision has tilted the NBA's media axis: ESPN, having abandoned all pretense of honest journalism by giving LeBron total control of the network to revel in solipsistic lunacy, now has a Superteam to pimp, and its spanking new Heat Index will devote more resources to covering the Heat than the rest of the league's teams combined.

It makes business sense: ABC/ESPN and the NBA are multibillion-dollar bed partners, with the league as the submissive bottom. The Miami Heat are going to be the new face of the brand. An ESPN reporter, Ric Bucher, is working on a LeBron book, too, and while he doesn't sport a Chief Wahoo tattoo, he does boast an NBA credential.

My only loophole requires that I work with the Heat media relations office, where another Tim—Tim Donovan—lets me know straightaway that "the fact that the book you are planning is not something LeBron signed off on does not play in your favor." I am free, however, to apply for credentials on an assignment-by-assignment basis, provided that an *Esquire* editor details each assignment to Tim Donovan's satisfaction.

. . .

OUT THE HOTEL room window early the next morning, waiting for the sweetest three words in the English language—"room service breakfast"—a line of clouds scuds low across the blue horizon. Tugs pull a huge cruise ship out of the bay and toward the sea. I can see a white crescent slice of the arena where the Heat play. It's a pretty picture, a glorious morning. Miami, I decide, is fine by me.

This may be the truth talking, or this may be the Vicodin. Hell, it may be both.

Fifteen years of living sober; fifteen years without a drink or a hit or a line; fifteen years avoiding all pain meds. In 1999, after a root canal, I filled a scrip for Oxycontin syrup, took a teaspoon of it over the kitchen sink, and when I felt it land in a warm rush pouring down as slow and sweet as honey, I tipped the rest of the bottle down the drain. Not because I worried I might relapse, but because I *knew* I would.

But the root canal didn't hurt as bad as my back does now. I'd slipped a disk three weeks before, on a Friday night—just bent over wrong and felt the lightning rip across the width of me. When I managed to slide downstairs, humped in two, limping, my son saw me and started to cry. Sorry, kid. Sorry you didn't know me when I was younger, tougher, and wholly unfit to be anybody's dad.

Lisa wanted me to go to the ER to get an injection. Fuck that. I slept in the rocker over the weekend, called my doctor, and he phoned in prescriptions for Valium to relax the spasms and Vicodin for the pain. I couldn't crawl to the crapper, let alone travel to Miami, without meds.

I'm taking half-doses, calling or texting Lisa every time I drop a pill, not because I'm worried that I'll relapse, but because I *know* I will. Never had a Vicodin in my life—we had Percodan back in the day—but with the very first one it's as if I never stepped away from the warm glow of the high. Put another log on the hearth. Stir the soup and heat me up a big bowl. I'm *home*, motherfucker.

SAUSAGE AND EGGS and a bagel and lox and a large pot of joe, and by the grace of God, I manage the drive to the arena without plunging into Biscayne Bay. I meet up with D-Wade at the team's offices inside the arena. He's wearing a black T-shirt with "NERD" in big white letters.

He seems friendly and relaxed. I've always liked him, as a fan. I liked the way Wade looked at LeBron at the moment when James started yapping about how easy winning was going to be: sideways, with his eyebrows cocked, a look that said, Slow down, son, I've *won* a championship. It wasn't easy.

Thanks for making the time, I say.

"Oh, no," Wade says. "You as well. Thank you."

It's a beautiful city. I get it.

He laughs. "You get it," he says, then laughs again. "It's a nice city."

I'm from Cleveland.

"*Oh.* You're from Cleveland."

The Q ain't gonna be the same, Dwyane.

Again he laughs. But he's nervous now, not smiling. We'll get to the standard stuff soon enough. And I'm not going to ask him any questions about LeBron. I'm a man of my word. But I have a couple of bones to pick.

Being a fan is ridiculous, I say. When you're a fan, you're stupid. Guys come and go and you're the idiot whose heart gets broke.

"I understand," he says. "I'm a fan of the Bears, not an easy thing. Sometimes you just get angry at guys—I understand that. My time in Miami will come and go. Another guy's gonna come in, but that fan stays the same. There's fans in the arena now watching me who'll be here 30 years from now watching someone else. And if they haven't won another championship in the next 30 years, they're gonna be feeling it, and I'll be sitting back like, Well, I won mine. I understand that."

Hating Dwyane Wade won't be easy. Doesn't drink, doesn't smoke, no tattoos.

No tattoos?

"I went one day when I got to college. When I was growing up, we couldn't wear hats, we couldn't wear earrings, my father said no tattoos. So I started wearing hats, and I got my ears pierced, and I said I'm going to go to the tattoo parlor. I walked in there and I walked right out. It just wasn't me—and I knew it wasn't me. It would've been forced."

Wade's summer has been packed—recruiting James and Bosh, flying back and forth to Chicago, where he was locked in legal combat with his ex for custody of their two sons, filming phone and shoe ads, shooting hoops and noshing shrimp at the White House.

"It was just like a big picnic on the lawn. Carmelo, LeBron, Chris Paul, Magic Johnson, Alonzo, Bill Russell—everyone sitting out there talking, Luther Vandross playing in the background. Just a great vibe."

Bill fucking Russell. I don't say this to Wade, but Russell's book *Second Wind* ought to be required reading for every NBA player and executive, not to mention every so-called journalist covering the league. Publicly addressing issues—sex, drugs, and, above all, the racism of American sport and society—with ferocious honesty and singular insight, Russell is the truest prophet pro sports ever produced, so wise that he long ago chose to absent himself in toto from the meaningless screaming clusterfuck of the national discourse, sporting and otherwise.

You know *Bill Russell?*

"He's a great man. The funny thing is, last summer we were golfing together—me, him, and Alonzo. I don't know how to golf, but it was an unbelievable opportunity for me to go out there and golf with one of the greats, right? And I can't hit the ball, and he's making fun of my swing, and I'm getting frustrated—Alonzo pulled me aside and said, 'Man, you're playing golf with *Bill Russell.* How many people can ever say they've done that?' I looked at him and said, 'You're right.'"

Cool. Very cool. But I'm still not rooting for you this season.

Wade nods, once. His smile is kind, indulgent.

"No one likes change. We'll be the Yankees of basketball. It's already true, but you know what? We're fine with that—we did something that *we* wanted to do."

AN HOUR LATER, Wade's behind a long table set up on a podium in a room full of press. LeBron sits to his left, Bosh to his right. The Heat have been consistent and careful: in every photo, poster, public appearance, D-Wade is the man in the middle, the sheriff flanked by his new deputies, still the centerpiece of the Heat.

Utter bullshit, of course. Three hundred or so members of the press aren't here because Dwyane Wade chose to stay in Miami, much less because of the ethereal Chris Bosh, who has spent his NBA days toiling in Toronto and is known best for having been dismissed as "the RuPaul of big men" by Shaq after Bosh whined about Shaq's low-post bullying in 2009. Everyone's here to see LeBron.

Especially me. I've shaved my Santa Claus beard—

Lisa missed my dimples, which apparently are more pleasant to behold than the adipose cascade of the rest of me—and I have no idea whether James has any idea who I am, regardless of how many times we saw each other last season in Cleveland and at Cavs' road games. I sit in the front row, make sure that my Chief Wahoo tattoo is in his line of sight, and stare at him. His eyes dart each time ours meet. Scowling, he strokes his beard.

I haven't been this close to him since I was in the Cavs' locker room, since I told him he was the best basketball player I'd ever seen, and I'm undone by my rage. Seeing him up there in his Heat uniform, I know that in a world of pure will and no consequences, I'd pay to have him knee-capped, with no sense of guilt at all. And at the same time, I know that this says far more about me than it does about LeBron James.

"For me, I've moved forward," he says, answering a question rendered inaudible by the fire roaring inside my head. "I don't want to dwell on the past. There's been a lot of things said about me, about my family, but I'm moving forward."

All three—decked out in their pristine home whites, sitting like schoolboys in front of a bunch of morons with their tape recorders and laptops and notebooks—look like they'd rather be somewhere else, but only LeBron, grim and frowning, looks pissed off. His obvious discomfort makes me happy, makes me hate him all the more. I want to stand atop my chair and shout, *Smile*, motherfucker—this is what you wanted.

"It's funny when things happen in life, and how people react," LeBron says. Again, I've missed the question. "It seems like a lot of people try to tell you what to do with your life—and most of the time they don't even have their own life in order, and that was just funny to me."

Ah—he means Dan Gilbert's letter, right? He couldn't possibly be referring to me.

"I went home and I been home," James is saying. "I been home all summer, still standing tall. Hasn't been a problem."

Standing tall, my ass. His annual Bike-A-Thon in Akron was cut short; a source at NBA headquarters told me that the league was concerned enough about his safety to send their own security folks to the event. He was booed in New York City as he entered the church to attend Carmelo Anthony's wedding; booed and mocked at the ESPYs, where he was a no-show; taunted at Cedar Point—an amusement park in Sandusky, Ohio, an hour west of Cleveland. The movie he was supposed to star in, a basketball comedy, was shelved after The Decision. He's a motherfucking pariah.

Bosh has hardly spoken, and Wade has grown increasingly silent as question after question goes to James. Bosh, long of neck, walleyed, may as well not be there. Wade turns in his chair, lips pursed, looking at LeBron.

"All this hero-villain mess is bizarre," James says. "You guys know me—I study the history of the game. That's what the league was back in the day. You had three or four All Stars—you had two or three Hall of Famers—on the same team. That's what this game is all about. I'm gonna go out and let my game do the talking."

I heard your game last May, LeBron. It said, No mas. You choked, you quit, you ran. I really ought to grab one of these folding chairs and smash your skull.

Not good, I know. Homicidal ideation rarely is a sign of quality sobriety. I'm a dad, a husband, a pillar of society. If I'm in an uproar like this in a room of sportswriters over a ballplayer, the player can't possibly be the real problem.

Fred Exley: that's who flashes through my mind. Exley was a great writer—*A Fan's Notes*, a barely fictional memoir of a raving New York Giants fan, is his best work by far—and an awful drunk. He drank away his talent, then he drank away his life; he died in 1992, 63 years old.

Much of *A Fan's Notes* details his obsession with Frank Gifford, which began at USC when they both attended school there. Gifford was all that Exley wasn't, all that Exley's father, a local sports legend in Watertown, New York, wanted his son to become.

Exley's love for Gifford was profound, gut-wrenching, hilarious, and frankly insane. Exley himself was nuts—much of the book is about his time in the loony bin—and filled with a self-loathing refined unto purity by a life spent not just failing, but endlessly fondling each failure. The man forgave himself nothing and boozed until he drowned his voice, which failed long before his heart.

But I'm not thinking of *A Fan's Notes*; I'm thinking of

Exley's second book, the sadly inferior *Pages from a Cold Island*, required reading for writers who wake up with shaking hands and no clue what comes next on the page. Toward the end of that book, Exley recalls a fan letter from a shrink who, deeply moved, tells Exley "he had never before encountered a man so haunted by sense of place."

I have met such a man. His face fills my mirror every time I brush my teeth.

Behold this spoiled pissant basketball player who imagines that he's standing tall because he took a televised shit on Cleveland and somebody with nothing to lose has yet to cap his silly ass. Strength, Lord. Give me strength.

WATER. I need water. I need another Vicodin. My lower back is clenched so tight, I can barely lift myself off the chair.

One of the interns herding the Heat to the basketball court to tape short one-on-ones with the local broadcasters kindly brings me a small bottle of water. I fish the pill bottle out of my briefcase.

I'm calling my wife now. As ever, I get rolled into voicemail. I try the landline. Nope. I try her cell again. Nada. Landline. Cell. Landline. Cell. Landline. Cell. She is unavailable. Unreachable. I miss her. I want her to be there for me every time I want her to be there for me. I want to whisper into the small pink shell of her ear that as our years together have unfolded, the mystery of our love grows ever more unfathomable, especially the mystery of where the *fuck* she is or why the *fuck* she doesn't answer her *fucking* cell phone. I leave a message:

"It's me. You're probably upstairs banging the Poland Spring guy. I just took a Vicodin. I saw LeBron. Now I need to find Z. It's almost three—try to get the Poland Spring guy out of the house before the boy gets home from school."

Inside the arena, I spot an intern.

Has Z been in here yet?

"I'm sorry?"

Mr. Ilgauskas. Tall Lithuanian chap?

"I don't think so."

I grab a sideline seat and watch and wait. LeBron's on a folding chair in front of a white screen being interviewed by a local TV guy—one of a half dozen, each with his little setup and cameraman—looking miserable. This is the crap he'd refuse to do in Cleveland, but Dwyane Wade is the Man here, and Wade does it, so King Shit can't ditch the media. Not yet, anyway.

I see Z come through the runway, all seven pale feet and three inches of him. Zydrunas Ilgauskas, drafted by the Cavs in 1996 out of Kaunas, Lithuania, is one of the most deeply loved athletes in Cleveland sports history. The bones in his feet started fracturing early in his career, after he signed a $70 million contract in 1998. He had surgery on both feet and missed three entire seasons, and he kept rehabbing with no guarantee he'd ever play another game in the NBA, and he did this even though he could have quit and still been paid all of the money owed him.

The Whore of Akron asked Z, also a free agent, to follow him to Miami, promising a championship, and Ilgauskas signed with the Heat for slightly more than $1 million. But Z also did something else: he bought a full-page ad in the *Plain Dealer*:

Dear Cleveland,

When I came to this country 14 years ago, I was a young man who barely spoke the language and had no idea what to expect of this great country.

As I look back on those early days, I realize how lucky I was to have grown up in a place like Cleveland. All of you have taught me the importance of family and friends; of pulling together to get things done; of loving your country.

I've never felt as proud as when I've pulled on the wine and gold and stepped onto the court.

I've tried my best to return that support by playing as hard as I could each and every game.

The decision to play for Miami was not an easy one to make for either myself or my family.

But as I enter the last few years of my career, I

felt I owed it to myself and my family to chase my
dream of winning an NBA championship.

I hope you understand.

I also hope you realize that Cleveland will
always be home to me.

With Love and Appreciation,
Zydrunas "Z" Ilgauskas

For Cleveland sports fans—and the proper analogy
here isn't the heartbroken ex; it is the wife who has been
beaten to the kitchen linoleum over the course of decades
and who cowers there, trapped, helpless, soul sick, and
condemned forever to a marriage of cosmic suffering—
Z's love letter was unprecedented gallantry.

Between interviews, Z comes over to talk. We got to
know each other a little bit in Cleveland last season, and
seeing him now in a Heat uniform makes my chest ache.
Although that could be the Vicodin. Or arterial plaque.

You miss Cleveland, Z?

"I do, yeah. It's hard, you know, after fourteen years.
I'm a Cleveland guy."

The knot in my throat stops my voice. My eyes fill
with tears. Z puts a huge hand on my shoulder. Gently,
he squeezes.

Z, what happened against the Celtics? What the fuck
happened?

"I think they were just a better team at that point.

They just beat us. They played great. I think that we were not in the right mind-set—if we looked toward Orlando or the Lakers, or we thought we were better than we were. We just kind of thought we were going to show up and everything's going to be okay. So for us—we were in a dogfight, and we weren't ready for it."

Were you shocked when he decided not to come back?

"Yeah. I always thought that Cleveland was probably going to be the destination. I'm sure that he did, too, when it all started."

I'm writing a book. About him. I'm upset with him. Very, very angry.

"Tell him that," he says, laughing now. The intern comes over to escort him to the next interview.

I'll be back, Z. I hope we can talk more. For the book.

"Sure. It's good to see a friendly face."

Off he lumbers, a huge man in his work clothes. I hunt down Tim Donovan, the Heat's media relations head, to thank him for the credential. A little bridge building. It's the polite thing to do, the smart thing. Long season.

As soon as I introduce myself, it's clear that Tim Donovan has sized me up, found me wanting, and won't waste time pretending to be anything other than what he most enjoys being: a gimlet-eyed prick. To his credit, he isn't buying any of my bullshit about our mutual love for New Jersey—he lettered in lacrosse at Rutgers—and couldn't care less about my gushing over how gosh-darned excit-

ing the coming season will be. He can barely bring himself to shake my hand.

"Yeah," he says. "Great."

Tim has been a Pat Riley henchman for fifteen years,
going back to Riley's Thug Life Knicks. Maybe Tim sniffs
Jew or despises slob. That could explain the way his upper
lip curls and his wedge of prematurely gray hair bristles.
His white shirt is bone-white, fitted; his tie is knotted
small and tight at his throat.

"I have a lot of work to do," he says.

Do I blame Tim for his rudeness? *Au contraire*: I prize
his clarity. Better to deal with a prick than a merchant of
smarm. He will make me a more resourceful journalist,
and I will soften and cajole him, wend my way into his
heart. We'll be pals by season's end; I can feel it. Although
that could be the Vicodin.

CHAPTER SEVEN

THIS COULD BE
THEIR YEAR,
SCOTTY!

Immediately after Media Day, the Heat leave for training camp. In a stroke of singular genius, Pat Riley holds it at Eglin Air Force Base—500 miles from Miami, where the team trained in the pre-LeBron era. Apart from all the sports pap about team building and discipline ("It also presents us a unique and fantastic opportunity to spend time with the airmen who defend our freedom," Heat head coach Erik Spoelstra said), it is a calculated fuck-you to the press.

Everyone, including beat reporters who'd covered the team for years, is required to complete a two-page affidavit, subject to a federal security check. Bring your own phone and online access or do without. The players' lodging is on the base itself, inaccessible to the media, whose members catch a bus each day from a checkpoint to be brought "directly to the gymnasium" at Hurlburt field.

Brilliant. I fill out the form—including full disclosure of tattoos, even the arrowed heart with MOTHER in its center—and tell Donovan I hope to profile Riley for *Esquire*. No interest, Tim says, which truly grieves me.

I admire Riley. An Irish lad from my wife's neck of upstate New York, the son of a pro baseball player whose hope of becoming a major league manager ended in booze and ashes, Riley's career spans most of modern basketball. He played for Adolph Rupp at the University of Kentucky (Riley led the all-white UK team that lost to Texas

Western's all-black team in the 1966 NCAA Championship), and after nine seasons in the NBA, mainly with the Lakers as a backup guard, he had gone on to coach both the Lakers' Showtime ballerinas and the Knicks' pug uglies before blowing New York City for Miami in a typhoon of tampering charges—*plus ça* fucking *change*—that wound up costing the Heat a million bucks plus a first-round draft pick. Riley became, en route, a tricoastal *face*, a perma-tanned, Armani-draped, gel-haired operator who pulls down fifty grand a pop as a motivational speaker. If the visionary king of the ancient Celts, Red Auerbach, ever had a true heir, it is the shrewd and ruthless Riley.

INSTEAD OF ENLISTING at Hurlburt, I fly to Chicago for my brother David's son's bar mitzvah, the first such family event I've attended in a decade, maybe more. Dave and I often go years without speaking to each other. We're not feuding; we're busy. But everyone's busy, and I've long since come to believe that the years we spent in our grandparents' house did too much psychic damage to smooth over or undo. The shitstorm inside those walls poured downhill same as everywhere else, and Dave was often the victim of my anger and my fists. Too often.

What we have now is an unspoken understanding based on mutual trauma. We don't talk because there's so much left to say, and it would hurt so much to say it—and it wouldn't change a thing. Long ago, we went our separate ways.

Still, you don't blow off a brother's son's bar mitzvah. I just wish I weren't in such lousy shape. My lower legs and feet have ballooned to the point that I can't get my shoes on. I've been diagnosed with lymphedema, an embarrassing diagnosis for a roughneck like me. Women who've had breast cancer surgery get lymphedema. In my case, it's from forty years of losing and gaining back 50, 75, or 100 pounds over and over.

Lymphedema is the good news. The bad news is, I weigh 380 pounds. Worse: My doctor recommends the South Beach Diet, proving once more that for a Cleveland fan, there is no justice—only irony.

What was it LeBron had said about people taking shots at him whose own lives weren't in order? I go to Chicago with my legs and feet wrapped tight in compression bandages, wearing a pair of size 15 Crocs, feeling more ashamed by the way I look than scared by the shape I'm in. I don't ever doubt my game: I'll drop the weight; I'll deal with the Vicodin. I won't relapse and I can't die. Not on a wife whose voice on the phone is enough to make me hard in my hotel room, not on a son who counts on me, and, by God, not before fulfilling a sacred mission. All of which makes me hungry.

∙ ∙ ∙

FOR MANY YEARS after Art Modell moved the Browns to Baltimore in 1995, I tried in vain to convince the Ravens' media relations people to let me profile him. Their front office peope were too smart to ever say yes. Maybe I would've throttled that kike bastard. Or maybe we would have wept together over the parcel of rue each man is doomed to drag to his grave.

I was past forty when I began to make real money as a writer, but real money couldn't make a good writer out of me, much less a good man. To me, the struggle to write well and the struggle to manage my alcoholism and addiction and weight and insanity are all battles in the same war. I am not the man I want to be. Being that man isn't possible—and it doesn't matter. What matters—pardon my mitchalbomania—is the effort. A man never quits, makes excuses, or points fingers.

My dad didn't teach me any of that, by the way. Cleveland did.

LEBRON IS NOT MODELL. He is far worse—a native son who betrayed the fatherland. But James also is in many ways no more than an ill-schooled doofus who saw *Gladiator* and thought it was the greatest movie ever made. He named his second son, Bryce Maximus—his firstborn was LeBron Junior, of course—and so had WHAT WE DO IN LIFE tattooed on his right bicep, and

ECHOES IN ETERNITY on his left. He is more cartoon than man.

Which makes me . . . what, exactly? The night before I fly to Chicago, as Lisa creams and wraps my swollen legs, I think of Nicky, who hasn't crossed my mind since 1983. I was working nights at a nursing home; I punched in at four, watered the flowers, then drove the van up from the back lot to take the day-care crowd home. Nicky rode shotgun, my last drop-off, a sweet, stubby man in his late twenties who had Down syndrome.

Nicky worked part-time in the occupational therapy workshop in the nursing home's basement, lived with his parents, and loved the Cleveland Indians with a steady hope that brooked no doubt or discouragement, despite the fact that the team had by then been comatose for more than twenty years.

I started hating Nicky in mid-February, when pitchers and catchers reported to spring training.

"They look good this year, Scotty," Nicky would say. Always "Scotty," which drove me crazy—no one ever called me that.

Spring training, Nicky. Doesn't mean a thing.

"This could be their year, Scotty."

All I wanted to do was get him to his parents' place, smoke the bone sitting in my front pocket, and kill a little time driving the scenic route back to the job.

No way, Nicky. They'll finish sixth again. They suck.

"Could be, Scotty."

This goes on every day and word for word. I want to scream at Nicky that he has no idea what he's talking about, that he knows less than nothing about the subject—that they have been a bad, boring ball club for years and always will be—but at this point I just shake my head and squeeze the steering wheel.

"You never know, Scotty."

I know, Nicky. Trust me, I *know.*

"It's possible, Scotty."

It *isn't* possible, Nicky. They're not good enough. They're a *terrible* team—that's *why* they finish sixth every season. They *stink.*

"This could be their year, Scotty."

Never do I pull the van to the curb, slam it into Park, and clock Nicky square in his mongoloid grin, but I think about it daily. I visualize rearing back, throwing my right hand, and watching his face cave in. When I drop him off, I'm grinding my teeth and he scrambles down from his seat, a man at peace with the world and himself.

"See you tomorrow, Scotty."

THERE ARE LEG wraps and foot wraps, and tan support hose that go on before the wraps. There is my wife on her knees. Not so many years ago, I weighed 200 pounds and a handjob was what I gave myself when I was on the road—a few times while on the phone with Lisa talking low about what she'd be doing to me if I were home in bed with her.

The man I used to be is in here somewhere. I don't miss him right now, recalling Nicky. I don't miss burning with blind rage at a young man with a small child's brain. Whatever his deficits, Nicky was the perfect—nay, the Platonic—Cleveland sports fan. I have no idea if Nicky's still around, or if he and I will live long enough to see the season he thought every season could be. No matter. Nicky *believed*—and believing was plenty good enough for him.

IN THE WAKE of the Whore of Akron's leave taking, Clevelanders were too blind in their rage to articulate their loss—and the sportswritters were too blind to begin to understand the source of that rage. I'd hear or read tripe like this, from *Dime* magazine:

> The getting-dumped process is going pretty much according to plan for the Cleveland Cavaliers. First there was the emotionally irrational behavior (burning LeBron jerseys the night of "The Decision"), then the period of pretending like you didn't want to be with your significant other in the first place (Dan Gilbert's open letter), then the optimism when you remember there are other fish in the sea

(only the Cavs couldn't get any of them to take the bait), and finally the cosmetic payback work—new wardrobe, losing weight, better car, etc.—to make the one who dumped you feel like ass the next time you meet. Hence the Cavs' new uniforms that were unveiled yesterday to a mixed response.

Over and over, ad nauseam, everywhere.

Never mind that many of the same sports journalists spouting this nonsense were at least dimly aware that there was an entire planet full of fanatics who had just spent a month following the World Cup with a fervor born not of romantic love, but of something far more powerful and transcendent: love of country, of home, of blood.

Never mind that ESPN, whose greed has reduced its journalism to self-parody, produced and broadcast a documentary, *The Two Escobars*, wherein the coach of Colombia's national team told of how a nation with a long history of losing at soccer was transformed by overnight success:

"They said, 'That's our team—our identity.' They embraced us and infused us with the joy that is the heart of our people. We manifested their dreams, ignited their passion.'"

Never mind that around the world, a single soccer, cricket, or rugby match can capture and embody a whole people's history and self-regard, and change it as profoundly and permanently as war.

Never mind that the best basketball player in the world, born and raised in northeast Ohio, had quit in the playoffs and then quit on the city, yet still wasn't quite satisfied with the wreckage.

"We hated Cleveland growing up," LeBron said to one writer after The Decision. "There's a lot of people in Cleveland we still hate to this day."

No perfect analogy exists for the disgrace and dishonor Cleveland fans suffered with LeBron James's collapse against the Celtics followed by The Decision, but to reduce it to a high school prom queen dumping her *zhlub* of an old boyfriend was ignorance, pure and lazy.

No one in the national media even tried to examine the larger cultural and historical issues at the heart of the matter. Like anything else more complex than a car chase—climate change, health care, terrorism—The Decision itself was nothing but fodder produced by and for benighted fools capable of grasping only the simplest narrative.

I have known romantic love, requited and un-; I have been dumped, rebuked, and scorned; I have nursed such hurt a long time sometimes—indeed, sometimes for too long. But this is not that hurt. I love Cleveland with a patriot's heart, not a schoolboy's.

So excuse me for hoping that the Whore of Akron blows out a knee at Hurlburt. Or, better, both knees. Because if I have learned anything from watching this beast, it is that he is as near to indestructible as any athlete ever born. Also because if I have learned one lesson from the long malaise of Cleveland fanhood, it is this: LeBron and the Heat are bound for glory.

GOOD TO COME to Chicago. Good to have the Vicodin with me. Good that the old man, who'd made stupid noises about flying in from Los Angeles, didn't show. Plundered and abandoned by his Gypsy, he had gone through two months of depression, until he found a Filipino woman to move in with him. He called one Sunday morning to say he was in love. I told him I know that story by heart, and asked about his meds.

"Fuck you," he said.

"No, fuck you," I said, and hung up, knowing he'd be aces for another few months, until the Filipino took what she needed and went away.

My mother is a different kettle of herring. All you need to know about Lucille Friedman Raab Mandel Michael is that husband number three was a happy-go-lucky clarinet player named Erwin, a mellow Jew her age, whom she had dated once in high school. Erwin had lost his wife and buried a son and beaten cancer himself. He had never met an obstacle he couldn't overcome until he became Lucille's man, a condition he endured for a matter of months before jumping in his car one day and taking his talents back to West Palm Beach.

She sees me at the shul in Chicago—morbidly obese, limping, literally bent—and I know her inner Shelley Winters is dying to bust loose. I know too that she can't make a real scene without my help, which for the first time in memory I refuse to offer.

Instead, I tell her I know how I look. I'm working on it, I say. Don't upset me. Don't upset Lisa. Let's enjoy ourselves.

Dayenu. It works. A fucking miracle. We shall mark the date each year, and celebrate with rugelach and Vicodin.

At the Kiddush lunch after the ceremony, I see her from afar, the woman who bore and raised me. She's almost eighty now; I'm almost sixty. LeBron loves Gloria; I have mixed feelings about Lucille. My first tattoo is forty years old, the heart with MOTHER bannered across it, meant as a parody and to piss her off. I got it in 1971. Not so many years from now, we'll both be dead. Players come and go but no mother will ever replace her. The Browns, Cavs, and Indians will live on. Not her.

There will be other Cleveland fans eating their livers season after losing season. Not me.

It feels like half an epiphany, which may be worse than no epiphany at all.

Worse still: no lox.

There is lox, mind you, just not for a 400-pound Jew.

Better a whole Vicodin than half of an epiphany.

Fuck you, LeBron.

CHAPTER EIGHT

HATER DAZE

I land in Cleveland under the same sunless sky I left in May. Heavy weather coming. My bones know it. I smell it on the north wind. I grew up on this reservation.

The Cavs open tomorrow at home against the Celtics, who open tonight against the Heat. The guard at the car-rental parking lot gate was an usher at the Stadium on December 27, 1964. John. Eighty years old, a big-fisted ramrod. No one is a stranger to me here. I head for the Great Swamp Erie and follow North Marginal Road along its shoreline—past the municipal power plant that boy-mayor Dennis Kucinich refused to hand over to the bankers and monopolists who bled Cleveland dry, past the concrete pier that for many years pleaded "Help me. I'm dying. L. Erie" in shaky spray paint—and pull to the curb on a block of East 72nd Street. It was always a rough block. The graffiti on the rail bridge span above and across it featured in my day a swastika under the legend "White Power"—but now it's glass-littered, half abandoned. I gaze up to the blind second-floor windows where the bedrooms of the Sisters Zimmerman, German goddesses of my early twenties, used to be.

Kelly worked occasionally as a topless dancer; Char, the smart one, was my first great love. Both are long, long gone.

"You can't find any Jewish girls to date?" my mother used to ask.

I didn't like Jewish girls, and even if I had, I didn't know any Jewish girls looking for a tattooed college dropout who broke into vending machines for pocket money. Maybe I should have looked harder. Maybe somewhere in Beachwood or Shaker Heights my naked Jewess awaited, bent over a mirrored dresser, with a couple of 'ludes in her palm and a pint of Jim Beam.

Then away. From East 72nd back to the lake and up Liberty Boulevard, which now is named for Martin Luther King, snaking through cultural gardens planted after John D. Rockefeller bequeathed the land before the Great War. There is ghetto on both sides of the road, up the hill, beyond the trees, out of sight. Just off Liberty is where Big George bought me my first Polish Boy—kielbasa with fries, slaw, and BBQ sauce on top—paid for with the coins we had plundered from the dorm's vending machines.

I WATCH THE Miami-Boston opener alone in my room at the Residence Inn. The Heat look glum and play tight. James scores 31 points but turns the ball over 8 times in an 8-point loss. The Celtics fans boo him all game, hard. When he's at the free-throw line, some of them wave sticks stapled with a photo of Delonte West's face; West has signed with Boston, but he's sitting out the season's first ten games as a league punishment for his weapons arrest last season with the Cavs.

It's a bitter sight to watch LeBron playing for the Heat. Tomorrow night at the Q, the lights will dim, flames will belch from the JumboTron, the packed house will come roaring to its feet, and 20,562 people spurned by a home-grown god will stare down upon the corkscrew curls of Anderson Varejao. Who, by the way, would like to be traded.

At least Cousin Jeff will be there. He'd sell the seat, if only he could find a buyer. I don't need it: I'll be back in the highest perch on press row, up where the Chinese guys used to sit. They're gone, too.

AT SHOOTAROUND ON the morning of the Cavs opener, Joe Gabriele introduces me to old Jim Chones, a shambling 6'11" mountain who works as a postgame radio analyst for the team's flagship radio station. Chones is only three years older than I am; he seems ancient only because he has been twenty-six years old in my head for the past thirty-five years, ever since the Miracle of Richfield.

The Miracle of Richfield was not a shot or a game; it was a team and a season, an unfolding of fate that can stand alone as an exemplar of the cruel architecture of Cleveland sports. The Cavs were in their sixth year of existence and their second year of play at the Coliseum. They began the 1975–76 season with some reasons for optimism: they had finished the previous year a best-ever

40–42; they had a nice core of versatile young talent and a few steady journeymen; and they were led by their original coach, Bill Fitch, a former Marine Corps drill instructor and savvy hoops tactician who would go on to coach a total of 27 seasons in the NBA.

They got off to a lousy start. Their best young player, Austin Carr, had suffered a serious knee injury the season before and would never fully get his game back, and Fitch had no leaders on the floor. On November 27 their record was 6–11, and they made what seemed like a minor trade, shipping a couple of feckless young centers to the Chicago Bulls for a backup forward and what was left of Nate Thurmond.

Thurmond was an Akron native and a monster of an NBA center with the San Francisco Warriors for most of his career. As a rookie in 1963, he had backed up Wilt Chamberlain on a Warriors team that lost to Bill Russell's Celtics; three seasons later, Nate averaged 19 points and 21 rebounds to lead San Francisco back to the finals, where they lost to a Philadelphia 76ers team led by Chamberlain. Thurmond was a punishing defender, an able low-post scorer, and still ranks fifth all-time in rebounds per game.

By the time the Cavs got him, though, Nate was thirty-four years old and in his thirteenth season. His cranky back and knees limited him to 20 minutes a game, and he was averaging 4 points and 5 rebounds for the Bulls. In short, he was shot.

But something wonderful—something approaching

alchemy—happened when Thurmond arrived. Fitch actually played Nate fewer minutes, but Thurmond's experience and smarts made for a deep Cavs squad, one that could rotate two separate teams depending on the game situation and opponent. Thurmond led a backup unit that could choke off any offense the Cavs faced, and young Jim Chones, in his fourth season, led a starting five that was efficient, if not spectacular, with the ball in their hands.

After Nate Thurmond joined the Cavs, their record was 43–22. Ten players averaged more than 15 minutes per game; seven averaged double figures in scoring. They were a joy to watch for a fan, not only because they won, but because the pleasure they took in playing with one another was infectious.

The Cavs clinched the NBA Central Division, made the playoffs for the first time, and the Coliseum was all of a sudden filled with 21,000 fans calling down lightning every night they played. They faced Washington first; the Bullets had finished one game behind Cleveland and started three future Hall of Famers—Wes Unseld, Elvin Hayes, and Dave Bing.

The series came down to a Game 7 at Richfield, and Game 7 came down to one play. Dick Snyder, one of the Cavs' vets—and a native of nearby North Canton—took an inbounds pass with nine seconds left, faked a pass, dribbled twice, drove past Unseld toward the basket, and laid the ball up and in with four seconds on the clock.

The Bullets inbound pass from half-court was a lob toward the basket; Snyder knocked it away. Phil Chenier of the Bullets grabbed the ball in the far corner and fired up a prayer over a leaping Thurmond. Never made it to the rim.

All at once, from every corner, thousands of fans rushed the court, mobbing the Cavs, hugging each other, thrusting their arms skyward, and finally tearing down the baskets. It is one of the greatest moments in Cleveland sports history, which means, of course, that it was followed quickly by one of the worst.

As the Cavs prepared to meet the Celtics for the Eastern Conference championship, Jim Chones came down on a teammate's foot at practice and broke his own foot. And that's how the Miracle of Richfield ends. Nate Thurmond is forced to play without a backup against the Celtics' Dave Cowens, a future Hall of Famer in his prime. The Cavs lose to Boston in six games, the Celtics go on to beat the Suns in the Finals, and I will never meet a Cleveland fan who won't insist that the Cavs would've won it all if not for Jim Chones's broken foot.

Including Jim Chones.

"No doubt," he says. After Chones was traded to the Lakers in 1979, he won his title, and on the night he won, he thought back on the Miracle of Richfield and wept, and said to himself for all of Cleveland: "*We* should have won the championship."

Some Cleveland fans still rank the ending of the Miracle of Richfield at the top of the list of heartache. I myself don't have a list. I don't need a list. But I think it says something profound about the experience of Cleveland fanhood: what Clevelanders refer to as a miracle ended in heartbreak and agony.

Frankly, Chones would rather talk about his writing—three novellas, he says, and forty-six short stories.

I'd prefer to talk about LeBron.

"If you were raising a child," says Chones, "would you always give that child *everything* he wanted?"

Of course not. But what the hell befell the guy last year in the playoffs? How did he come apart and take the whole damn team down with him?

"He became what he always was," is all Chones says.

Back at the Residence Inn, I pull Chones's business card out of my wallet and toss it on the desk. On the back, it says "Writer-Philosopher."

LEBRON IS EVERYWHERE, and nowhere. Nobody wants to speak of him. Even poor Mo Williams, who admits that he considered retiring rather than facing life without LeBron, avoids the subject now. Dan Gilbert calls him "the player who left."

One beat writer asks Gilbert if he's making a conscious effort not to speak his name.

"Who's 'his?'" Gilbert replies.

Behind the closed, unmarked door of the owner's suite directly across the hall from the locker room, the nicest thing Gilbert calls him is "The Queen."

"It's still a shock," he says. "I can't believe he actually did this. It's just unreal. He fucks the entire city and then on top of it dances on your grave—it's unbelievable. There's no words for it—the amount of rage."

I find myself thinking that the only cold-eyed businessman in this sad farce was James himself. LeBron knew the business long before the Ping-Pong balls delivered him unto Cleveland. He had dealt with the shoe companies. He had gone to court to restore his high school eligibility. He had seen Gloria James and Eddie Jackson hustling cash for years based on his future earnings. He saw Maverick Carter drop out of college to take a job offered by Nike as part of the company's yearslong wooing. LeBron was a pro long before he graduated high school.

When LeBron joined the Cavs, Gordon Gund owned the team, by all accounts a fine man, a civic giant. Gund had gone blind at age thirty, but rarely missed attending a home game in person. He watched through Cavs' radio announcer Joe Tait's voice in his earphones.

Carlos Boozer played his second season when LeBron was a rookie, and they made a formidable pair. Boozer, a power forward from Duke, played close to the basket and angry. He averaged double figures in points and rebounding, and James's first-year numbers were better than all but two rookies in NBA history: Oscar Robertson and Michael Jordan.

They had Ilgauskas at center. They had a tough, experienced head coach, Paul Silas, who won three rings as a player, one of them as an enforcer on that Celtics team that beat the Miracle at Richfield Cavs back in 1976.

Those 2003–4 Cavs won 35 games—they'd won only 17 the year before—and missed the playoffs by one game.

It hardly mattered, because the Cavs were bound for glory. Every Cleveland fan saw it coming each time LeBron did something on the court no one had ever witnessed before.

Then Carlos Boozer, in the off season, walked away from a handshake deal with Gordon Gund and signed with Utah. The Cavs had him under his rookie deal for a third season at league minimum. They let him out of that commitment with the understanding that Boozer would immediately ink a new contract with Cleveland. Carlos still claims he never gave Gund his word. Maybe he had his fingers crossed and Gund never saw it.

The following season, Gund sold the team to Dan Gilbert, and Gilbert fired Silas with 18 games left in the season and the Cavs in the running for a playoff spot. They lost 8 of their last 12 games and ended up missing the playoffs by one game. Again.

That's when Gilbert hired Mike Brown and Danny Ferry, and began spending hundreds of millions of dollars on free agents, on upgrading the arena, on building the new practice facility, on trying to make sure that LeBron would never, ever leave.

How strange, how brutal, how infuriating it must be for Dan Gilbert to discover that the Whore of Akron's heart was never, ever really here.

THE CAVS HAVE a new slogan: "All for one. One for all."

Could be a season too late, is what I'm thinking. I want to stay positive; it's the opener. The crowd is great—not just enthused, *defiant*. We're still here, turncoat. You're gone? So what.

"We can't guarantee a whole lot of things," says Byron Scott to the fans before tip-off, standing in front of the team at center court. "But one thing we can guarantee is we'll get a maximum effort from these guys behind me, who'll play hard every single night."

The crowd goes apeshit. I can't begrudge them their excitement just because I'm not feeling the love, nor can I force myself to muster the same optimistic spirit. I know too much. I have been here too many times before, with every Cleveland team. I have paid my dues over and over, living and dying with bad, boring teams stocked with has-beens, never-weres, and clowns.

But I'll be damned if these Cavs don't come at Boston hard, with more than a little defiance of their own.

Down by 5 after three quarters, they run the Celtics off the court in the fourth. Sure, Boston's old, and tired from last night's thrashing of the Heat, but when the confetti starts falling from the rafters and Dan Gilbert is high-fiving everyone he can reach, it doesn't really matter. I am well pleased.

In the locker room afterward, Joe Gabriele yells over the din at me.

"Your favorite commercial's on."

It's Wieden & Kennedy's new "What Should I Do?" spot, starring the player who left as the iconic rebel who must go his own way, whose smoldering integrity simply won't let him live by anyone else's rules. Something like that.

"Gutless motherfucker," I bark at the screen.

Boobie Gibson, backup guard, looks wide-eyed at me.

"I'm sorry," I say. "Did I say that out loud?"

He cackles.

A man I've never seen before walks up to me, sticks out his hand.

"I'm Wright Thompson. We've never met, but we have a lot of mutual friends."

Wright has choppered in to work on a story about Cleveland after the apocalypse for ESPN's website. He turns out to be a good guy. We go to a nearby bar. I show him my ticket stub. I tell him the story of Ray Chapman's grave, or try to. I start crying before I can get to the part about all the coins.

Maybe it's the Vicodin. Maybe it's the win over the Celtics. Or maybe I've stepped back through the looking glass.

I'm here. I'm home. I'm circus-fat and soft in the head; already I stink from the road. I miss my wife. I miss my son. I've got a plane to catch in the morning, to Miami, and a date with the Whore of Akron tomorrow night.

CHAPTER NINE

JEW OVER MIAMI

have inhaled a half pound of unsalted jumbo cashews by the time I squeeze into the single-seat row of an MIA-bound commuter jet built in Brazil. No first-class section. One bitter flight attendant, whom I accost.

I seem to have outgrown my seat belt.

She is as pleased to hear this as I am to say it. Perhaps I should've said, Jumbo *c'est moi*.

A hundred pounds ago, on a plane from Florida to Newark, a flight attendant leaned over to ask Jumbo if he was married. The sweater and slacks he wore that day still hang in his closet, waiting to be bagged with the rest of the flotsam that will follow him to hell.

Now? Now flight attendants look at Jumbo and think about where the defibrillator is stowed. At such moments as this—asking for a seat-belt extension—no one can possibly loathe Jumbo Cashew as much as Jumbo Cashew loathes himself.

Jumbo is not the only passenger on his way to the Heat game. Adrift on this morning's Vike, Jumbo can't be certain that the entire posse is aboard—but that tall rumpled gent in a track suit a few rows back is certainly Lynn Merritt, LeBron's Nike shadow, the same jamoke who strong-armed the dunk tape last summer. And the handsome young fellow with the fade in the seat in front of Jumbo—could that be Rich Paul, one of James's Akron friends and business partners?

Jumbo hopes so: he would hate to be inflicting this searing flatulence, ripe with last night's burrito and guacamole, on a complete stranger.

At baggage claim, I spot Lynn Merritt and ask if he knows of an extra singleton to the Heat opener tomorrow night. My question is for sport and also serious: I requested credentials from the Heat more than a week ago, but Tim Donovan hasn't yet seen fit to answer yes or no.

Merritt eyes Jumbo with surly amusement. Despite our paths crossing last season outside the Cavs locker room before and after a score or more of games, he is either unable to place the silvered land walrus in front of him now, or unwilling to proffer a hint of recognition. His smile is tight, disapproving, as if he finds my presumption that he is in town for a basketball game insulting.

"You can't afford to sit where we sit," Merritt says.

How much?

"Twenty-five thousand dollars. But they're not for sale."

You must be sitting next to LeBron.

"That's right."

Merritt hauls a mammoth Nike duffel off the carousel and wheels it away.

Jumbo's Samsonite is heavy with Luna Bars. A rented Malibu, a bed at the Marriott Biscayne Bay, plenty of pills: Jumbo on the loose, riding high. Maybe too high to drive. He takes refuge in a Starbucks. The face of the barista there carries him back to the tiny village in

Ukraine where John Demjanjuk was born, where Jumbo interviewed a one-legged nonagenarian farmer who had been Demjanjuk's boyhood chum and whose granddaughter looked just like Bobby Kennedy's daughter Kerry and the airport barista.

Her feet were dirt-crusted, her thighs firm, her smile sunny. Beaming, she showed him two piglets squealing in the barn, but Jumbo could hear a deeper snuffling close by and beseeched the interpreter to ask Kerry about it. Kerry giggled, and drew with her outstretched hands the shape of the creature hidden by a low door at the side of the barn, then opened the door to reveal the Shaquille O'Neal of hogs.

Something she says makes the interpreter laugh.

"You remind her of the sow," the interpreter says.

Jumbo tells the interpreter to ask where the nearest Jew is buried.

The interpreter shrugs, one hand raised, puzzled.

THE GUARD AT the rental-car gate says he knows someone selling tickets to the Heat game, and he writes his phone number on my Thrifty envelope. I can't even remember the drive to the Marriott. I make a mental note not to take the Valium together with the Vicodin.

I can use a nap. I can always use a nap.

I wake up to find two new e-mails. The one from big

Z says he has family visiting and won't be able to meet with me while I'm in town. The other one is from Tim Donovan: "We can't do tomorrow. Sorry."

That's each and every word, and it took the dick 10 days.

Fine. Good. I'll buy a seat. I'll get the postgame sound files from my pals on the beat. I'll make do. I believe firmly in sports journalism's Second Law: A $40 room-service cheeseburger plate will fix any problem.

I also worship the First Law, of course: Everything that happens is good for the story. It may not be good for the story you're working on—the pig in Ukraine never made it into the Demjanjuk feature—but life is neither a magazine feature nor a book: life itself is the story whole.

In other words, if you wish to truly *taste* the room-service cheeseburger, you must first savor the smell of Tim Donovan's ass.

What Kerry Kennedy of Dubovi Makharyntsi saw when she looked at me helped teach me what Lynn Merritt saw at baggage claim, what Tim Donovan saw at Media Day. It isn't what my wife and son see—I'm not sure about the dog—and it isn't any insult to my pride or dignity. I have no pride, no dignity—I have a mission.

And I have a cheeseburger.

And a creed:

What another sees in you will reveal that person. What you see in another reveals your self. We are—each of us and all of us—mirrors.

• • •

IN THE MORNING, a fruit plate. With yogurt. And Vicodin. And a large pot of coffee. After I dine, I set up shop at the desk and scan the Heat's website, where hundreds of season-ticket holders are auctioning their seats to tonight's game. I nab one in Section 119, near center court, eleven rows from the floor, mine for a mere $546.25.

I crawl back into bed with the Heat's media guide, 444 pages of arcana. I'm stopped cold by a sentence on page 5, upon which is inscribed the biography of the Heat's owner, Micky Arison:

"Although his father, Ted, brought the NBA franchise to South Florida in 1988, it has only been since Micky took control in 1995 that the HEAT has evolved into one of the NBA's top organizations."

A son's sweet tribute to his dear, departed dad. Ted Arison was the founder of Carnival Cruise Lines, a Tel Aviv–born *gonif* who parlayed refurbished ships, slave labor, and tax evasion into an empire worth billions of dollars—so much *gelt* that in 1990, Ted renounced his American citizenship and moved back to Israel in an effort to avoid taxes on his estate, only to die in 1999, the world's richest Jew but nine months short of the IRS requirement that he live for ten years outside U.S. territory prior to his demise. An unlucky clan, clearly.

Even so, Ted somehow managed to leave Micky in decent enough shape for a billionaire, with Carnival and the basketball team and various other holdings, which is what makes Micky's media guide honesty so refreshing. Rather than brag about his old man, Mick tells you up top that Ted was no good at running the team, and then he never mentions his father again.

When it was time for me to go to college, my mother cosigned a government loan. My father said he was sorry that he couldn't help me out. I don't feel bad for myself; I feel bad for Micky Arison, who never had the chance to fail and find out who he really is, and who'll never forgive his dad for that.

I PICK UP my ticket at Will Call and watch a thunderstorm roiling above Biscayne Bay. The sky blackens, the wind gusts, the lightning crackles. In a minute or two, a wall of fat raindrops sweeps the street alongside the arena, and then moves along, leaving the air thickened, sticky warm. My shirt is soaked with sweat and rain. Toxic, this weather. Fat men keel over, their lungs full of syrup, their aortas burst, in this sort of sauna. It could happen, Scotty.

Some whiskered lout waves me over as I approach the stairs to the entrance. Jesus, he looks like a version of me that never got sober or grew fat as a pregnant sow. His name is Jack Subwick. He left Cleveland for Florida years ago and settled in Boca Raton. He doesn't have a ticket, says he doesn't care about the game, but he has opening-night programs for the Heat's whole life span, and asks me to pick one up for him and bring it back out.

I tell Jack to give me his number and I'll grab him a program and call to arrange delivery. Jack mulls it over briefly, then scribbles his number on the back of a restaurant coupon he yanks from his pocket.

Two missions.

It turns out the Heat have printed three covers of tonight's program—one with Wade, one with Bosh, one with James. I take one of each.

On his cover, LeBron glares into the camera, head lowered, eyes hooded, tight-lipped, his thick white headband riding ever higher on his forehead as his hairline approaches oblivion. He stands with his hands on his hips, with his shoulders thrust forward, the visual embodiment of his summertime tweet:

"Don't think for one minute that I haven't been keeping mental notes of everyone taking shots at me this summer. And I mean everyone."

He's ready to wreak havoc upon the NBA. No prisoners. Blood on the hardwood. Mano a mano. If your name's on Bron-Bron's list, you're going down hard as a motherfucker.

That's the pose. I think back to a game his rookie season, against the Indiana Pacers, when NBA tough guy Ron Artest was mugging James as he fought for position to take an inbounds pass. Artest had an arm across LeBron's upper chest and neck and a leg planted between James's knees bowing him backward. Paul Silas was coaching the Cavs, and Silas came up off the bench screaming—first at the nearest referee for not calling a foul on Artest, and then at LeBron for letting Artest unman him.

James has grown stronger and smarter over his seven seasons in the league, but he still tries to finesse defenders like Artest. His game has never hungered for a battle, much less marked him as the cruel-eyed enforcer who glares out from the program's cover.

GOD *DAMN,* it smells great in here. This has to be the best-smelling sports venue I've ever walked through. Bars everywhere, but the food grilling is what makes my nostrils twitch. Cuban chicken chop-chop. Arepas. Empanadas. It is a heavenly smell, and nearly enough to distract the brain from the women.

Nearly, I say, because god *damn,* the women are fine. Dark hair, darker eyes, dark skin and plenty of it. Liquid they strut, supple brown legs and heart-shaped asses, teeth agleam, the peals of their laughter melding into the stew of aroma, wafting high a soft yielding cloud of spice and sizzle and samba and sunshine and everything that Cleveland, Ohio, is not.

This doesn't even feel like a sporting event—it feels like a party to which I have never been invited.

God *damn*, it *is* a party: the arena itself is nearly vacant. I find my seat, an excellent seat, and study a two-page spread in the front of the program—"FAN UP, MIAMI!"—devoted to instructing Heat fans how to act like actual fans. Beginning with a Rileyesque us-versus-them taunting—"They say that Heat fans are fickle fans," that "Heat fans don't deserve to have a team like this," and that "It's time to prove the naysayers wrong"—it promises freebies and discounts to fans who get to their seats for tip-off and stick around for the whole game.

Lord. *This* is where LeBron James wants to play basketball, in front of sun-dried cretins who must be bribed to act like they care about the game and the team. Where another superstar already is the Man in the locker room and on the court; where nobody in the media will ever mention his collapse against Boston, his phantom elbow pain, and his steadfast refusal to hold himself accountable for his team's big-game failures.

For as long as I've been a fan, I've rooted hard against certain teams and players, but never have I hoped to see a career-ending injury—until tonight.

MY SEAT HAS a face value of $150 and is one of four owned by Dr. Jeffrey Rosen, who had been hoping to get $2,500 for it, and then $1,500, and then $1,000. Jeff does a nice job of pretending not to be disappointed, and

I restrain myself from embarrassing him by shouting at LeBron during warm-ups. Five minutes before tip-off, the lower bowl is barely half full.

A dreadlocked old man walking with two canes makes his way to a stool at center court. The PA announcer says that this is Clarence Clemons, which I find hard to believe. Only a little while ago—August 8, 1975—I saw Clarence Clemons for the first time, at the Akron Civic Center. I walked around the building afterward, snuck through the stage door, and thanked Bruce Springsteen for the greatest show I'd ever seen. Behind him stood the Big Man holding a fifth of Jack Daniel's, laughing as he drank—lit from within, he seemed like the coolest cat on the planet. I walked over and shook his huge, hot hand.

Twenty-five years later, from Rosen's seat, I watch the shrunken Big Man rest his back against the stool, pluck his sax from its stand, plant wide his feet, and blow a slow, shimmering anthem, each lush, lonely note a requiem.

Then the court is cleared for takeoff. LeBron is introduced first, Wade last. The choreography is painstaking; at one point, each of the three mega-super-duper-stars stands alone in a separate spotlight, hulking at the crowd. It feels like a Friday night opening of a Michael Bay movie, like a roller derby or pro wrestling match, fiction based on a true story, with an all-star cast. ESPN has raised a canopied porch in a section above one of the tunnels. Magic Johnson sits there perched on Magic Johnson's ass, an igloo of flesh.

The game is a 96–70 walkover. Orlando played its home opener last night, and Dwight Howard seems to be the sole Magic player with any want-to tonight. By the time he fouls out, the Heat are coasting and half the fans are empty seats.

James plays a swell second-banana's game—15 points, 7 assists, 6 rebounds—and at no point suffers a career-ending injury. With the game decided, he spends a good chunk of the second half on the bench biting his nails, an old habit he discarded in Cleveland. Only 78 games to go until the playoffs, 40 of them right here in Mojitoville, where the fans need an instructional manual to operate themselves, where the team fired its 30-person ticket sales staff after its season tickets sold out in July, and where the owner's son takes a piss on his dead father's pant leg to make himself look like a *macher*.

Welcome to Pippenhood in the tropics, putz.

MY CABBIE DOES not wish to take me to the Marriott Biscayne Bay, because he does not want to fight the arena traffic in that direction—a more rugged trip, it seems, than his recent journey here from Haiti. As we debate without any hope of understanding a word the other says, I get a text from Wright Thompson inviting me to the Mandarin Hotel bar. This suits the driver's mood; he nods when I show him the text and the $20 bill in my hand.

The Mandarin is apparently ESPN's headquarters for tonight's extravaganza. Wright is hunkered down at a long oval table across from John A. Walsh, the *eminence blanche* of the Worldwide Leader, the near-blind seer sprung from Scranton, Pennsylvania, American capital of coal dust and Catholicism, whose soft genius has helped shape American sports journalism for decades.

It was Walsh during his days at *Rolling Stone* who sent Hunter S. Thompson to cover Super Bowl VIII in Houston, Walsh who was founding editor of the fabled *Inside Sports* magazine in 1979, Walsh who gave birth to *SportsCenter*, Walsh whose encompassing beneficence has kindly touched hundreds and thousands of careers, including my own.

Walsh introduces me to his wife and son, and asks after my boss, who worked with Walsh many years ago. Couldn't be better, I say, and we sit beaming at each other.

Walsh is seven or eight years older than me and looks worse than I feel—wispy, dwarfish, his white beard sparse, his hair all but gone, his eyes rheumy—and god knows what he can make out of whatever he can see of me. We have always been fond of each other—Walsh because he adores lunatic writers, I because editors who enjoy lunatic writers are somewhat rare—and our acquaintance has never been sullied by having to work together or see each other too often.

Wright Thompson is talking about our meeting in the Cavs' locker room two nights ago, which I began, after he introduced himself, by telling him how much I have grown to despise ESPN. Hearty laughs all around.

Wright is a burly young man from Mississippi, a born storyteller. He's not trying to embarrass me—impossible in any event—or get a serious conversation started. The Heat game is over; ESPN's work here is finished; it's time to kick back, relax with a few drinks, and tell stories.

July 8 was one of the worst days in the history of Cleveland sports, I say. And that's no mean achievement.

More laughs.

At that moment, Michael Wilbon stops by to pay his respects. Wilbon's one of the many newspaper writers Walsh has helped groom into a television personality. I can't hear what Wilbon's saying as he leans over Walsh, but he's red-eyed and unsteady on his feet.

Wilbon goes, replaced by Dan Le Batard, the colossus of the Miami media market. Dan writes a column for the *Miami Herald*, does four hours of afternoon radio five days a week on the local ESPN affiliate, and pops up frequently these days as guest host on a couple of ESPN-TV shows. Dan's a good guy. He put me on his show one day last week, and he also put in a good word for me, way back when, with Tim Donovan. Given my chemistry, or lack thereof, with Tim, I probably owe Dan an apology, just for tainting him by association. I get up and walk his way, waiting for a quiet moment to take him aside.

I'm sorry, Dan. I know you vouched for me with Donovan, and I hope I haven't given you cause to regret it.

"That's fine," he says, but he sounds disappointed, even miffed. Dan cuts a fine figure in his black suit and white shirt, a man about town on opening night. I'm wearing a bright red Marvel Comics T-shirt with the Flash stretched tight across my apron of fat.

"Take it easy," Dan says. "You need to think about preserving access. Keep your ammunition dry for the book."

Walsh waves Dan back to the table, and they take a short walk together. Dan bends close to Walsh, who has one hand on Le Batard's biceps: the old master and another protégé are talking business.

I like these people, but I loathe ESPN, yes. I don't know if Walsh played any role at all in The Decision, but he is an executive VP, executive editor, and chairman of ESPN's editorial board.

When a young ESPN writer on the West Coast posted a story in late July about LeBron cavorting with his Akron crew and Lynn Merritt at a Vegas nightclub—carefully noting James's six-figure appearance fee and his taste for tequila and women without underwear—ESPN yanked it off its website in a matter of hours, explaining later that it never should have run because the reporter had failed to properly identify himself as such, and denying that James or anyone associated with him had anything to do with the story's disappearance.

Now ESPN is throwing money and bandwidth at a new brainchild: the "Heat Index," a full-court phalanx of reporters and columnists paying daily homage to the primacy of a single NBA team even as the vast bulk of news coverage of the entire league is dominated and driven by ESPN, which pays the NBA a billion dollars a year for broadcast rights and in turn derives huge profits from the ad time it sells to Nike and all the other companies who are themselves paying hundreds of millions of dollars in endorsement fees to the athletes ESPN's newshounds are paid to cover. Which obviously has nothing whatsoever to do with ESPN pulling a story about LeBron James acting the fool at a Vegas nightclub. *Obviously.*

Whatever John Walsh might choose to call it, this isn't credible journalism. It's a daisy chain.

No one with any sense will ever again consider ESPN an honest source of NBA coverage—but if anyone in charge at ESPN or the NBA cared about that, The Decision would never have aired. One ESPN executive said after July 8 that the network expected to have a one-on-one with LeBron as the season approached. The World Wide Leader got what everyone in Cleveland got the past seven years: *bupkes.*

CHAPTER TEN

THIS WAY
LIES MADNESS

Hating is a full-time job. Home from Miami, I sit in the rocker with two TV trays in front of me, one for my laptop, the other for my dinner. When Cavs and Heat games conflict, I watch Miami on the television, with my laptop tuned in to the Cleveland game on NBA.com's LeaguePass. The boy and I used to watch *The Simpsons* and *The Office* from seven to eight o'clock before he'd start his homework; now I'm watching a game or the pregame show on NBA TV. Google Alerts for James and the Heat arrive hourly, around the clock. I'm phoning sources in Cleveland, in Akron, in Miami, Los Angeles, New York City—I am building a one-man bureau: the Hate Index.

Twitter is now my drug of choice, a wormhole to a digital zoo where two hundred million animals fling feces at the wall and each other in 140-character chunks. Here I find players, among them @KingJames, and fans and journalists and even a few NBA team owners, such as @CavsDan, wandering in and out of a fractured gabfest that never ends.

On November 2, the Heat clock the Timberwolves, the Cavs lose to the Hawks, the Republicans kick the crap out of the Democrats, and I'm hard at work on Twitter lambasting the #WhoreOfAkron, taunting an *Orlando Sentinel* writer—a very nice man—for making fun of New Jersey, and dreaming out loud of a three-some with the Pope and Peggy Noonan, Twitter-drunk.

I GET ON the bike every day. I pull on my sweatpants by leaning against the bedroom wall, dangling them low because I'm too fat to lift a leg more than a few inches. To get my socks and shoes on, I have to use my arms to pull my foot up and rest it on my knee, and then I have to get the shoe on quick or the force of my belly pressing on my thigh will push my foot right off.

I stay on the bike five minutes, then ten minutes, then twenty minutes. I bought the bike in Iowa City, in the 1980s, as part of that decade's weight crusade. Now it's here in New Jersey, up on the third floor, in my office.

No more sandwiches. No more swiping the kid's pizza crust. No more this, no more that. I go to physical therapy three times a week. The back is feeling better. I've stopped taking the Vicodin, although I've saved a few. Insurance. For the road. Just in case.

When Lisa rubs and wraps my legs, I look down and see what has become of me—what I've done to myself. I'm not sure that I would rub and wrap her legs under these circumstances. I am sure that this is what love is—not a feeling, not an orgasm, not an anniversary gift. Love is doing what has to be done to keep body and soul together when your beloved is falling apart.

Home from school, my son hugs me, steps back, and formally proclaims, with a sardonic edge all too familiar, that he can now touch his fingertips together when encircling my girth.

"Thanks, Oedipus," I say. "Don't pluck out your eyes on my account."

This boy. This miracle. To become a father at the age of forty-seven is to know how close I came to missing out altogether, to never knowing how much I could love and how much I could be loved.

How much more redemption and grace could a sane man possibly seek than this?

WHEN I LEFT Cleveland in 1984 for Iowa City, after the Iowa's Workshop let me in. I was thirty-two, without money or prospects. I never dreamed I would be gone so long. I thought I'd tear back home like Elvis, with a gold-plated Cadillac and a wad of hundreds in my pocket.

My first wife was turned down by Iowa's graduate biology program because her GRE scores made her look like a moron and her grades from CSU seemed like a joke without a punch line. It wasn't her fault: she was a Cleveland girl who went to city schools and chose the voc-tech track and went to work as a bank secretary while she was still in high school.

Then she realized that she was smarter than her bosses at the bank, and that being a secretary meant that she'd never be looked at as anything more than that, so she bulled through a year of remedial coursework at Cleveland State, which is where we met. She graduated with a 4.0, but the test scores and the Cleveland State University imprimatur killed her chances of getting a shot at a good doctoral program.

Didn't faze her. She was pure West Side, a funny, foul-mouthed Cleveland girl with a white trash mother from Snow Shoe, Pennsylvania, and a moon-faced pop who grew up in an orphanage on a Northern Cheyenne reservation in Whitefish, Montana. All you truly need to know of her—and of the steel in Cleveland's spine—is that she's a specialist at the Mayo Clinic now.

We were married for ten years and never really talked about having kids. I was always loaded, so maybe we did and I just don't remember. But it wasn't an issue, especially after she got into medical school. The amount of work was staggering, she was already past thirty, and the academic road ahead stretched for seven years or more. When she did her first ob-gyn rotation during her third year, she talked about how relieved she was that she wouldn't have to endure the act of giving birth.

What the hell did I care? When she got into medical school—after three years of lab work with the school's star research scientist, and six months of prepping for the MCATs—I was the drunken douche bag who'd just hit the lottery. Now I could stay loaded forever and write, which is all I ever wanted to do. I didn't buy her a Hummer with her future earnings; I bought myself a lifetime's free pass.

I CAN'T SLEEP. It's Monday, an off night for the Cavs and for the Heat, and it's past midnight and I'm up on the third floor but all I can hear is the whispering inside the refrigerator down in the kitchen. The boy's turkey bologna is in there, conniving with the sliced American cheese. The mayo's in there, too. Lisa just went shopping yesterday, so there's plenty. The kid won't miss it. Nobody has to know. The bread isn't going to talk: I'll take a couple of slices from the middle of the loaf.

It's not a good plan. It's not even a plan; it's a craving. Give it up. There's fresh fruit down there. Yogurt. Granola. Salad fixings. All the things Lisa eats. You can't fall asleep on an empty stomach? Okay: put some healthy food in there.

Feh. I want the sandwich. I want two or three of them. It is the alcoholic's credo: one is too many and one thousand is never enough.

I come up with a compromise: I'll take a Valium. It's past two a.m.; I'm not taking it to get high. I just want to get to sleep.

This is an excellent plan. The only problem with this plan is that I don't feel like taking the Valium and going straight to bed. I'll wait until the Valium kicks in, which shouldn't be long on an empty stomach.

It's an amusing thought, an empty stomach. Somewhere inside this massive sagging gut is the much smaller pouch of my actual stomach. Where's the Valium? Ah, it's still in the front pocket of my briefcase, in a little brown prescription bottle with the Vicodin.

Huh. Could be that this isn't such a good plan after all. Because with the little brown bottle in my hand, I no longer want just the Valium any more than I wanted just one sandwich. Let me rethink the plan.

IT TAKES NO more time to rethink the plan than it does to pour a glass of water in the kitchen and bolt the Valium and the Vicodin. The chatter inside the refrigerator has stopped. The dog looks at me. Smartest dog I've ever known. Fucker's smiling.

Who's the big puppy?

That get his tail going, all right. Besides, who the fuck is he going to tell. Smart as he is, he's still a dog.

"And you're still an addict," he says.

Actually, I say it for him.

I sit in the rocker, open the laptop, and sign on to Twitter.

First thing I see is a tweet from @KingJames:

"I love my chef B so much(pause)! He made the meanest/ best peach cobbler I've ever had in life. Wow!!"

James attaches a photo of the cobbler, which looks fabulous: two huge rough-cut hunks, gold-crusted and gleaming, with a couple of slabs of vanilla ice cream on top.

It's 2:30 a.m., and he has a game tomorrow night— *tonight*—against the Utah Jazz, and he's scarfing cobbler and tweeting about it like he's ten years old.

Can I hate the sinner and love the sin? I do.

"Note to self: Cobbler hard to hate," I tweet.

A minute later, "ESPN ramps up Cobbler Index," followed immediately by a third tweet:

"Broussard sez @KingJames having pineapple upside-down cake tom'w. Bucher doing recipe book. Wilbon to query chef. J Gray wiping Bron's ass."

By this time, the dog is laughing. By this time, I can taste the fucking cobbler. Oh, I could really use that sandwich. If only I could figure out how to get out of the chair. This slow rush of narcotic joy is a dear old friend who needs no invite to make himself at home. *Mi casa es,* motherfucker.

Reminds me: I'm overdue for my next colonoscopy, for those too-few seconds between the anesthesiologist unloosing the fentanyl-and-Versed cocktail and unconsciousness. Next time, I'll have peach cobbler after I wake up. Maybe they can find a way to get some cobbler into the IV tube?

The room spins and goes dark, but only for a second. When I lift my head off my chest, I see James's tweet, each letter of it throbbing.

What the hell does "(pause)" mean?

"You tell me," the dog says, tilting his head toward the recliner on the other side of the fireplace where my father sits reading the paper. He's in his thirties, back when he was my father, with a white T-shirt tight over his biceps and a short cigar stinking cheap.

When I was five or six years old, he sat on the front patio of our house behind a newspaper while I caught with my face the flying fists of Dickie Schwartz, the bully of the block. Sat there while I fought to keep my feet at the bottom of the driveway.

Ignoble prick.

"I was trying to teach you an important lesson: in this world, you have to fight your own battles."

You taught me something more important than that: expect to be abandoned by those you love when you need them most—just like Willie taught you.

Sandy raises the paper back in front of his face. The old *Cleveland Press*. The dog is gone. LeBron is sitting on the couch and he has a dish of cobbler for me.

"Is that what you're *going to teach your boy?"* LeBron asks. *"You're killing yourself with a fork and spoon."*

Jesus, this cobbler's beastly good.

"Haaaaa."

He's dressed like Urkel. I saw you in this outfit—a

cardigan over a plaid shirt, big black-framed glasses—at Madison Square Garden a year ago almost to the day.

"I scored thirty-three."

So young. Young enough to be my son.

"I was a father when I was eighteen," he says.

When I was your age, I took my talents to Austin, Texas. Tended bar and drank around the clock. Smoked weed coated with angel dust and dropped bad acid. Managed a 24-unit apartment complex with the girl I left Cleveland with—a sweet young Catholic poet from Garfield Heights.

"Why would you write about my cock? What's wrong with you?"

I don't know, kid. I thought you were staying in Cleveland when I saw your dick. You fucked up—you quit. You lied. You left.

"What does any of that have to do with my cock?"

Nothing. Not a thing. It just seemed funny, almost falling over the towel thing, looking over, boom.

"You should've stayed in Texas, man. Maybe you'd have grown up."

I had to leave. I rented an apartment to a woman whose boyfriend was an outlaw biker. She worked at a massage parlor. Austin was full of massage parlors full of young women turning tricks. Rotten Rod—her boyfriend—was essentially a pimp.

"Rotten Rod?"

That was his outlaw sobriquet. I just called him Rod.

We smoked the PCP. We played chess. As you might guess, his game was a tad aggressive. But he was good. His own father—a biker too—had taught him to play at an early age. He talked about his dad a lot. But it wasn't real friendship—he had no one else to talk to except Crazy John, and even before John got run over and killed on East Lamar, he was generally too fucked up to keep a conversation going. Not long after John passed—under the wheels of a semi—Rod suggested that I put my girl to work at the massage parlor, and I found myself at a loss. Could I say that I wasn't the kind of skunk who'd do that? He was trying to be helpful; he knew we didn't have much money. And I think he was looking for a partner.

"What'd you tell him?"

I told him she would never do it.

"What'd he say?"

He said, "If she loved you, she would." He said, "She wouldn't have to touch no Meskins or niggers." Something like that.

"What'd you say?"

I can't recall.

"You can't recall."

Man, this cobbler's tasty.

"You were scared."

Oh, you have no idea how scared. I was selling weed by the pound, to outlaw bikers. Not a good plan. They always paid, until they didn't. "My girl got crabs and had a lousy week"; "I had to spring for another rebuilt carbure-tor"; "I've got a road trip coming up." I couldn't collect. I had no leverage, no muscle. I knew it. They knew it. I couldn't pay *my* guy. I had to leave town quick. Not like you. Nobody gave a damn where I was except for the folks I owed money.

"That girl from Garfield Heights?"

Gone. I can't even recall why. I remember her little sister died in a car accident back in Cleveland. Maybe she left then. Maybe things fell apart before that. I was too fucked up to notice.

"How dare you judge me?"

You spit on millions of people.

"I don't answer to them. I do what's right for LeBron."

Is that what you'd tell a West Akron kid who cried when you left the Cavs?

"I spit on nobody. I played my ass off for seven years. Those kids never once heard of me with drugs or guns or any of that stuff. Not once. Those were the best years that team ever had, and you judge me for leaving like it's the worst crime ever committed."

I can't think of a parallel betrayal in the history of American sports.

"What's the worst thing you ever did?"

Summer of 1994. I got the woman I love pregnant. She was afraid to have the kid. I wanted the kid—I was forty-two years old, I'd destroyed everything in my life, including my marriage. I *still* wanted that kid. All she wanted in return was the promise that I'd sober up. Just the promise.

"*What happened?*"

I couldn't do it.

"*What happened?*"

She had the abortion. I drove her to the hospital myself. Drove her there, drove her home, went back to my place, got fucked up, got out my shotgun, and put it in my mouth.

"*What happened?*"

I couldn't do that, either.

"*You crying?*"

It's the cobbler, LeBron. It's the meanest/best cobbler I've ever had.

CHAPTER ELEVEN

LITTLE ACCESS
FOR A BIG MAN

never did kill myself. I didn't want the dog to eat me.

BARELY HAS THE plane to Miami taken off—half a minute, tops—when the dinging and the chiming begin.

"Way too soon," I say to the woman next to me. She's reading a book in Hebrew, which I had found reassuring before we took off. I don't know why that felt reassuring; I think it had something to do with being in first class. I'm in front of the little curtain for the first time in many years, having used my carefully hoarded One Pass miles. All is right in the world. Better than all right: I am *special*, and so is my life. A fellow Jew? Flying out of Newark, of all places? To Miami yet? *Quelle phenomenon!*

"What?" says the woman. "Too what?" Her accent is Israeli.

Too *soon*, I say. The dinging. The chiming. The bells. Something's wrong.

The captain gets on the PA to tell us that one of the crew has reported smelling "an electrical odor" in the back of the plane. Captain Landry says he is going to "vector" us back to Newark. I'm grateful he called us "folks" and gave us his name. Vector away.

The Israeli woman is on her cell phone. She's speaking Hebrew—Greek to me. Finished, she tells me that her husband's a pilot and he says our plane is on fire.

"El Al?" I ask.

No. He flies an F-15 in the Israeli air force. "What will happen?" she asks me. A worried Jew—imagine such a thing.

We'll be fine, I tell her. You're sitting next to me. And I am on a mission from God.

She laughs.

How calm I feel. No more Vicodin, no more Valium; I have flushed the pills down the crapper after my peach cobbler vision quest. I can't even credit first class for the depth of my serenity. I feel ready to face the fact of death. God I trust no further than I can heave my washing machine, but the Heat are struggling, *and* I have a son. I am complete.

Also I can tell from his voice alone that our Captain Landry is an ace, a major *sheygetz*. I see fire trucks racing along the tarmac as we land, but there is no fire. We debark in the usual manner, to cool our heels in the terminal while they fetch another plane.

I call home to tell Lisa I love her, and ask her to put the boy on the phone so I can tell him I love him, too.

Have I mentioned his name? I don't like to mention his name for the same reason that I find myself—it is a reflex, involuntary—saying *kinehora* each time I refer to him, just as my grandmother did when I was a child. No evil eye shall befall him.

People—stupid people—ask me if he's smart. Not the brightest bulb in the chandelier, I say. Never brag on a child. Don't assume or announce anything good. God or the Cossacks will get here shortly. Either way, the innocent and defenseless will be set aflame. The real suffering is always yet to come.

His name is Thomas Judah Brennan Raab. No hyphens. I hate when people hyphenate their progeny, as if two car dealerships had merged. I thought of maybe putting in a semicolon: Thomas Judah; Brennan Raab. Thomas Brennan was my wife's father's name; he died before I met Lisa. I wanted Judah in honor of Judah Maccabee, a Jewish farmer-warrior whose Old Testament prowess led to the recapture of the temple and to Hanukkah.

Judah is his name. Fruit of my loins. Light of my life. My kaddish, whose first full sentence was, "Fuck Derek Jeter." Perhaps not his first. But close.

THE MOOD IN Heatville is dark when I arrive, and the mavens who called the team a threat to win 65 or 70 games before they ever played a single one have gone silent. Three nights ago, Miami blew a 22-point lead at home against the Utah Jazz and lost in overtime, 116–114. LeBron posted a triple-double, but he shot 5–18 and failed to score a single point in overtime.

After the loss, Wade admitted that the Heat might have panicked, while James noted that Utah coach Jerry Sloan had Erik Spoelstra's plays figured out before the Heat ran them. Two nights later, James scored 35 points and missed a triple-double by one assist as the Heat lost at home to the Celtics, 112–107. Late in the game, LeBron clanked two free throws and a layup, then complained afterward that he and Wade had played too many minutes.

"For myself, 44 minutes is too much. I think Coach Spo knows that. Forty minutes for D-Wade is too much. We have to have as much energy as we can to finish games out."

The Heat are 5–4, and for all his talk of "getting to know each other," Coach Spo must already feel the cold edge of the dagger at his back. I can't think of another situation in any pro sport where a star free agent has joined a new team and begun the season by publicly criticizing his new head coach.

I've arrived in time to catch Saturday night's game against the hapless Raptors. I have beleaguered both Tims—Frank at NBA media relations and Donovan at the Heat—with e-mails detailing my plan to cover the final three games of this home stand and file a daily report on Esquire.com, and an *Esquire* editor has sent both Tims confirmation of my assignment, which conforms to their putative requirements for a media credential.

Tim Donovan's hand is forced, but only so far. He grants me a credential for tonight's game with Toronto. "We will let you know [about the rest of the week]," Tim says, after he "see[s] what [I am] reporting."

I CAN REPORT that the Heat fashionistas are having trouble finding the arena, and those who have do not wish to Fan Up! I see thousands of empty seats at the Raptors game, and the actual attendees, even in the lumpenprole upper bowl above which Tim Donovan has thoughtfully found a spot for me, do not fulfill the exhortations of the PA announcer, an unblinking toad who seems to have been left behind by the same alien craft that brought Chris Bosh to earth.

The second half of the game is like the first. The Raptors make a couple of runs, but lack the sort of conviction that a team with more talent might display. The Raptors clearly prefer losing with quiet dignity this evening to wasting energy on a cause lost before the opening tip.

Tim Donovan has found a unique way to control the postgame media throng: Nobody is allowed to speak with Bosh, Wade, or James in the locker room. They will appear "in the Media Interview Room at the conclusion of each home game."

It's not much of a throng—a couple of dozen guys who need to file a story about a 9-point Heat win of no particular interest. Spoelstra is first to appear. He's pale, hollow-eyed, clearly exhausted.

"It's good to get a win, obviously," he says. "That's the most important thing. And to continue the process of trying to build our habits and get better."

He sounds like Mike Brown. Like Brown, Spoelstra worked his way up from the video room. He's Pat Riley's golden boy, but now that he has Wade, James, and Bosh, the sports media—and not only in Miami—are wondering if he can deal with the pressure and expectations. No one has forgotten 2006, when Riley fired Stan Van Gundy after 21 games and coached the Heat to their only championship.

Bosh appears next. When he's asked about the pressure of facing his former team, he says, "I kind of worked through the nerves a little bit. We've been through so many nervous situations, my nerves really didn't get to me that much."

I make a note: "BOSH NERVOUS." The guy sat most of the game with foul trouble and was a nonfactor in the outcome. Shaq told me there were players who'd commit fouls on purpose some nights in order to get back on the bench as soon as possible. That's exactly what Chris Bosh looked like he was doing tonight.

Wade and James take the podium together. Wade answers the questions; LeBron is chewing gum. He stares down at the table. I'm sitting front and center, staring straight at him while Wade talks about the pressure on Coach Spo to win it all.

"We haven't executed the game plan," Wade says. "The coaches have done an unbelievable job."

LeBron looks up from the table. Someone has asked him a question about learning to play with Wade.

"We're both attackers," James says, looking like a man in prison. Where's the happy-go-lucky lad surrounded by his mates as he lifted his second MVP trophy last May?

"This is a process that we know only time will heal," he says, scowling.

Heal? Is he trying to tell me something? Has he a clue that the Jabba the Hutt–looking scribe front and center has trailed him to Miami, that I'm the same blob who was asking about Shaq and thanked him for being the best basketball player he'd ever seen? Is it possible that LeBron thinks I am one of many, sent on reconnaissance by a brigade of porcine Clevelanders, each marked with a Chief Wahoo tattoo?

I'm staring at the Whore of Akron. I'm not nodding or smiling or taking notes. I'm just staring. And he won't meet my eyes.

SATURDAY NIGHT ON South Beach, but I am on the far end of Collins Avenue, far from the glow. I have no stomach for the action. Sleep. Tomorrow morning I'll drive north on I-95 to Hollywood, Florida, to a bar where

I will watch the Cleveland Browns play the New York Jets nestled in the warm, yielding bosom of the Browns Backers Club, which has chapters all over the world, including Afghanistan and the West Bank, but not in Miami.

I'm at an old hotel, a three-floor job, a little run-down, but so am I. I'm awakened by laughter somewhere close by—laughter and the smell of good weed.

I'm not going out there. Not tonight, anyway. Tonight, I'll have a Luna Bar and seek succor in what is printed upon its wrapper, one of the "inspirational" woman-to-woman messages so cloying that they could've been composed only by a sardonic young gay man in a marketing department cubicle.

"To my grandmommy, who taught me that no mountain is ever too high! You are my inspiration and my hero! I love you!—Brooke."

I miss Gram. What she taught *me* is that most people, if you give them half a chance, will prove to be no brighter than farm animals and bent on malice. She was the *shtetl* in a white bakery smock, her varicose legs rotted with ulcers, covered in ointment, and wrapped—like mine!—with compression bandages to keep her from scratching herself open. When the itching got bad enough, she'd take a butter knife from the kitchen drawer and work it down under the bandage, where its blunt tip could provide her some relief. I can still see the bloody smear on the knife when she'd pull it out! My inspiration! My hero!

What's for dessert tonight, LeBron?

Here, motherfucker, have a Bratislava Bar!

I'M WATCHING THE Browns-Jets game with the Backers at Mickey Byrne's Irish Pub. I have my laptop open at a table as far as possible from the bar because Chimay Ale is known for its reach.

There are 30 or so Browns fans here. They all hate LeBron, naturally, but some have known worse. Mark Gudin was at the stadium for the final Browns game there—December 17, 1995—when the fans literally tore the old place apart seat by seat, and the police, fearing bloodshed, let them.

"Talk about ripping the soul," Gudin says. "It was like being at a funeral."

I was living in Philly then; I didn't want to go. I could not have borne it. I've watched the clips on YouTube; just *thinking* about what happened when that game ended makes me cry. The Cleveland Browns, unprompted, jogged downfield to the bleachers to say thanks and farewell, to hug and to be hugged by the Cleveland fans they never wanted to leave behind.

"I get goose bumps," Gudin says. "Those guys *got* it. And that's the big part about LeBron that makes me so angry—he just doesn't get it. And he should."

Watching with these folks is intoxicating. They're

loud and drunk, and the Browns are playing a great game, led by rookie quarterback Colt McCoy, who throws a game-tying touchdown pass with only 44 seconds left.

"Colt McCoy" may be the greatest name ever to grace an NFL quarterback. Colt McCoy once swam 300 yards to save a drowning man. Colt McCoy won more college football games than any quarterback in NCCA Division 1 history. And for a few minutes, here in Hollywood, Florida, I think I'm destined to see Colt motherfucking McCoy beat the Jets.

You'll never guess who else is watching the Browns-Jets game. Go ahead, guess. I'll wait.

That's right: the Whore of Akron sees the Jets marching in the fourth quarter and tweets, "Sanchez is wearing them down." And I fire back: "But they haven't quit. Look in the mirror, motherfucker. You're a fucking loser and always will be."

Then the Browns are driving for an overtime win when a Browns' receiver named Chansi Stuckey fumbles at the Jets' 32-yard line. The Jets score with 16 seconds left in OT.

All I want is to climb over the bar, bend backwards under the Chimay tap, open my mouth, and spend an hour swallowing. I'm not loving the mission. The mission is beginning to feel like unleavened misery. This Browns loss is a perfect distillation of the past 50 years of crushed Cleveland fanhood.

For a Cleveland fan, there is no *déjà vu*, no *presque vu*, no *jamais vu*; for us, it's all *vu*: everything known, understood in all its fullness in the instant when Chansi Stuckey, bucking for one more yard, has the football torn from his grasp.

O Nicky, where art thou? How could I have known then that what made me want to punch you in the face was the ineffable resemblance I saw there to my own? So many more seasons full of bitter, wrenching defeat, and still I sit entranced, the blood pounding in my ears, my fists clenched, my heart wide open—because after all these games and seasons and years, *this could be the game.* Would I still be living and dying with this bullshit if I didn't believe that it could happen, Nicky?

But it never does.

THAT NIGHT, I file my *Esquire* post and e-mail Tim Donovan requesting access to practice so I can spend a few minutes with Z, who seems less than eager to meet with me now. I assure him in our e-mail correspondence that I want only to sing his praises—the loyal Cavalier who left Cleveland "the right way" to chase a ring—and will not ask him about LeBron.

No need to ask Z. James is about to close on a $9 million estate in Coconut Grove. His girlfriend, who does not like Miami, is in Ohio with their sons. LeBron is here, partying hard.

LeBron does not like Erik Spoelstra, who has the temerity to confront him at practice when LeBron starts goofing. He does not want to play point guard. He does not understand why the fans are booing him everywhere the Heat play. He's a young man far from home, living on his own for the first time ever, and he doesn't seem happy.

I am not devoid of sympathy. I listen to the gossip and wish that I could help him focus on what truly matters in a man's life. It would take only a few words, and a tire iron.

Word comes from Tim Donovan at 4:01 p.m., a one-line e-mail:

"You are no longer welcome at our building and will not be credentialed going forward."

That's it. I send a reply at 4:04, asking why. Never heard from Tim Donovan again.

My piece blows up when it runs the next day. *New York Times* big. I'm not going to lie: When I see "Whore of Akron" in the *Times*, it feels good. It felt like the pinnacle of my fucking career.

Tim Frank at the NBA office even had a statement prepared:

"There's an expectation of professionalism on both sides in the team-media relationship, and the posts on Mr. Raab's twitter account clearly fall short of that standard."

Another NBA spokesman said I was still free to seek one-game credentials from other teams.

Tim Donovan told the *Times* that after I "used inappropriate language via Twitter directed at one of our players, we conferred with the league office and decided to no longer offer credentials to Mr. Raab for our games and practices."

Eh.

I buy myself a seat for Wednesday's game in the "Dewars Club" section, four rows up from the floor and right across from the Heat bench. It cost $278, but I get to sit so close to Pat Riley that I can smell the dirt in his casket. All in all, I don't feel unwelcome. In fact, I'm beginning to like Miami.

THERE'S A DINER of sorts across from the hotel called Big Pink. I set up there—I'm out of Luna Bars—and eat pulled-pork omelets, thick tomato slices with big wheels of mozzarella, and iced coffee. When you tip like I tip, you can pull out the laptop and spend a few hours on it. I've gotten to know a waitress named Taina, and Taina is cool with my professional loitering.

Taina has waited on LeBron. She claims James tweeted a picture of her—no lie: I found it on his time line—and that his tip was so big that she used it to pay for a photography course.

I still hate him, I tell Taina.

"I can tell that you do," says Taina.

I have a mission.

"I do, too. I need to stop drinking so much wine."

CHAPTER TWELVE

THE TRAITOR'S
ON THE FLOOR

If I had to rank my worst days as a Cleveland fan, January 4, 1981, would be the rankest. The Browns were trailing Oakland, 14–12, with the ball on their own 14 and a little more than two minutes left in a divisional playoff game. The field was patched with sheets of ice; the Lake Erie gale battering the open end of the Stadium had dropped the wind-chill temperature to 36 below. The gray sky was falling dark and 78,245 fans were on their feet, calling down one more miracle from the Kardiac Kids, the team they'd seen pull win after last-minute win out of its ass all season, led by their rag-armed, brass-balled quarterback, Brian Sipe.

With players on both teams slipping on every play and the Browns heading into the gusting wind, Sipe somehow drives the Browns 73 yards. With 41 seconds left to play and one time-out left, the Browns face second down and 9 on the Raiders 13-yard line.

A field goal will win the game. But because the Browns are driving into the swirling maw, and because the Browns' Don Cockroft, history's last straight-ahead NFL placekicker, has already missed two field-goal attempts and had an extra point blocked, and because these Brownies have danced cheek-to-cheek all year with Death and have come to believe that they are a Team of Destiny, head coach Sam Rutigliano calls for a pass play designed to produce a touchdown.

Red Right 88.

Brian Sipe, in the only NFL playoff game he will ever play, drops back, moves left, and sees tight end Ozzie Newsome, his favorite receiver, running right to left across the back of the end zone. Sipe heaves the ball into the wind. The wobbling football never reaches Ozzie. It falls, along with Cleveland's hope, into the arms of a Raiders' safety.

Sipe stumbles toward the sideline, into Rutigliano's fatherly embrace. Sam doesn't scream, "You San Diego surfer son of a bitch!" Nor, "Did I *not* tell you to throw the football into the fucking lake if no one was open?" To his vast credit, Sam Rutigliano is not the sort of man who'd ever say these things.

"I love you, Brian" is what Sam does say.

The thought of which, even now, makes me want to run Sam Rutigliano through a wood chipper.

I WASN'T AT the Stadium that day. I couldn't afford the ticket. I was living in a $75-a-month room in an old house in Cleveland Heights, after going bust as a weed dealer in Texas. Another boarder had a TV, so I watched the game in his room. When Sipe threw the pick, I headed down the stairs and out the front door. So cold, it hurt to breathe.

I didn't know yet about Rutigliano's "I love you,

Brian," and it wouldn't have mattered if I had: I wasn't capable of processing a single thought. The world stalled, with Sipe's final pass cast forever into the wind. I stood there empty, past tears, beyond words.

I could not know then that The Drive and The Fumble and The Shot and all the rest were coming down the pike. But even as those nightmares played out one by one, each a private sorrow and a public hell and all together forming a skein of unbroken, uninterrupted, apparently eternal misery, Red Right 88 hurt more because it came first. Nothing to befall a Cleveland sports team could ever pack the wallop of shock and disbelief I felt that day. Nothing could ever lay me so low.

NOTHING, THAT IS, until December 2, 2010, when LeBron James comes back to the Q. By now, the Heat are imploding and James is booed without mercy in every town they visit. Fans who couldn't care less about Cleveland or the Cavaliers saw The Decision and came to the same conclusion about LeBron: Asshole. Traitor. Egomaniac.

His defenders are quick to point out that all he did was exercise his right as a free agent. He hasn't been arrested for DUI or failed a drug test, wasn't charged with rape or pinched with a transsexual hooker. They don't understand that this is beside the point.

NBA fans *loved* LeBron. He was cheered almost everywhere the Cavs played, and even where he was hated—Detroit, Chicago, Boston, and Washington in particular—he was villainized for the right reasons: He came, he swaggered, and he kicked ass.

What they see now is a fraud. A brand name with no more substance than a marketing plan to move shoes and soft drinks. A self-proclaimed king without a crown, a blowhard who has been publicly disparaged by his iconic elders—Michael and Magic, Barkley and Bird—for lacking the esprit de combat that burned inside them and made them great. They don't question James's right to free agency or talent. They question his heart.

As 12/2 approaches, the Heat come close to cracking. They drop 3 games in a row, including a 16-point loss at home to the Indiana Pacers. On November 27, in Dallas, the Heat are on their way down again when Spoelstra calls a time-out and James, stalking back to the bench, bumps his shoulder into Spoelstra's hard enough to spin him sideways, something LeBron once did to Mike Brown, too.

On November 29, ESPN's top story leads with "The Miami Heat's players are frustrated with Erik Spoelstra and some are questioning whether he is the right coach for the team, according to people close to the situation." Spoelstra's offensive schemes are lame; he's too panicky about losing his job to be an effective coach; he's a lousy motivator who won't let his players be themselves.

The byline is Chris Broussard's; the fingerprints on the knife belong to Maverick Carter. It is an obvious assassination attempt and a message: LeBron holds himself blameless for anything going wrong in Miami.

I'm fairly plotzing from the pleasure of seeing the chickens so soon taking their talons home to roost. Another week of woe may force Pat Riley to rise from the tomb, thirsty for blood, and drain Eric Spoelstra's jugular.

How sweet it would be to see Miami hand itself over, as the Cavs once did, to the Whore of Akron. While the Heat go down in Dallas, the Cavs beat the Grizzlies in front of a full house at the Q on Saturday night—the same Memphis team that beat the Heat a week ago. Cleveland is a scrappy 7–10, and if the season ended today, they'd own the last playoff seed in the Eastern Conference.

Two nights before the Heat game, the Cavs lose big to the Celtics, but I write that off to the intensity of anticipation—all anybody's talking about, in Cleveland and everywhere else, is LeBronukkah.

GOOD TIMES IN the old hometown. Thanks to all the twittering and the hoo-ha after the Heat withdrew my nonexistent credentials, I'm now a local hero of sorts. There's not much competition. I'm feeling so buoyant that I invite my mother to lunch at the Cheesecake Factory, an act without precedent.

"What if they come after you?"

Who?

"LeBron's people."

What people?

"His friends."

Lucille's worried they'll shoot me. She's worried about my weight. She's worried about the thing on the side of my nose. "What is that?"

I don't know. A pimple?

"You need to get that checked. It doesn't look like a pimple to me—it looks like a mole or a growth. How long has it been there? I don't remember seeing it at Julian's bar mitzvah. Was it there then?"

This is fun, Mom. I don't know why we don't get together more often.

"I'm your mother. I worry about you."

You do realize I'm pushing sixty.

"What difference does that make? You will always be my child."

This stops me cold. I've heard it before, a thousand times, always as a curse, life without parole. Gloria James was sixteen years old when she had LeBron; Lucille was twenty-two when she had me. He has a tattoo of his mother's name in large cursive script; I have an arrowed heart with MOTHER in a banner across its center. Gloria borrowed against LeBron's future millions to buy him a Hummer; my mother repaid the shoe store while I was in London with the deposit bag, to keep them from pressing felony charges against me. I owe this woman far more than I have ever been man enough to acknowledge.

WHEN THURSDAY DAWNS, Cleveland feels like a city ready for a brawl. Pundits across the land, some local, keep warning fans not to give the town a "black eye" by burning down the Q. The natives, eyes permanently blackened by forty years' service as a media punch line and punching bag, are in no mood for lectures. Hundreds of media hypocrites have arrived here in force precisely *because* there might be violence. ESPN for weeks has speculated about the *likelihood* of violence. Most of the press here obviously *hopes* for violence—which, should it occur, they'll hold themselves blameless for helping to foment.

The big question is whether James will do his pregame chalk toss, and how the fans will respond. I offer the Cavs' media relations head $500 cash to allow me to stand between LeBron and the resin. I vow to maintain a strict policy of passive resistance, but I also assure him that James will not reach his target. He declines and also tells me that Dan Gilbert, whom I've asked to join for at least part of the game, is "too emotional" to meet with me now.

There are many more security guards than usual in the bowels of the Q, and there's a constant crackle on their walkie-talkies—LeBron has a code name: the Traitor. As in, "The Traitor's on the floor."

The booing that greets him when he comes out of the tunnel for the pregame shootaround unrolls without end. I can *feel* the sound in the pit of my stomach, although that could be the pair of Polish Boys I disappeared at lunch.

Then the chanting begins—"*ASS*-HOLE, *ASS*-HOLE, *ASS*-HOLE"—less dazzling but still inspiring in terms of its volume. The words "Merry Quitness" alternate with live shots of LeBron on the JumboTron as I squeeze my way up to Section 130.

When I pause to get my wind, a woman supervising the section checks the placard dangling on my heaving chest and bursts into tears.

"You're Scott Raab?"

I nod.

"I just want to thank you," she says. "Thank you for standing up for Cleveland. For all of us."

Please stop crying. Please. You're making *me* cry. What's your name?

"Chris. I was born in 1965," she says. "I have seen nothing but failure my entire life. I've been with the

Cavs for sixteen years, and I thought we were going to *finally* win something—*we're going to win something in my lifetime*—and then this piece of shit."

His name is unpronounceable; she simply points down to the floor.

"He's a piece of shit. He's never, ever going to be treated the way he was treated here."

The JumboTron's showing live shots of Cleveland heroes one by one as they walk to their seats. Drew Carey. Bernie Kosar. Josh Cribbs. Travis Hafner. The crowd cheers each face, but I find this parade heartbreaking. How little these urchins have ever had to celebrate. The last face on the screen is Dan Gilbert's, and his draws the loudest cheers of all.

James is introduced first, almost inaudibly. The booing turns to cheers when Ilgauskas is announced, but Z doesn't lift his head. Not so much as a wave: to acknowledge the Cleveland fans would be too great an affront to his lord, King James.

Eik nachui, Whore of Kaunas.

HE TOSSES THE CHALK. Of course he does. Now, who's going to toss a beer in his face from a courtside seat? I don't wish for mob violence, but I'd hoped that if James performed his routine as if this were just another arena, someone in the crowd would remind him—with a drink, a D-cell, a cinder block—that this is Cleveland, motherfucker.

Nope. And then, just before tip-off, the handshaking and hugging begin, and now the fans booing LeBron are watching Anderson Varejao embrace him like a long-lost brother. No hard feelings, LeBron—we don't really give a shit what our fans are feeling; we're all in the Millionaires Club, buddy. Let's just get this over with nice and easy. Please don't hurt us.

I'm booing in the press box, something I've never done before. I'm sick to my stomach. I don't even want to watch.

By the end of the first quarter, James has 10 points, 5 assists, and 4 rebounds. The Heat double Mo Williams as he brings the ball across mid-court; by the end of the first quarter, Mo has hit 1 of 5 shots and turned the ball over 3 times.

"AKRON HATES YOU," the crowd's chanting at LeBron as he toes the free-throw line. He's grinning ear-to-ear. The Cavs stand round-shouldered, arms dangling. Lambkins.

By halftime, the Heat are up 19. I walk down to the front of the press area to meet Cousin Jeff.

"Can you believe this?" he asks.

All my life, I say. All my life, whenever I've been stupid enough to think it won't get worse, it gets worse. Losing I expect. This meek surrender I do not. For the first time in my life, I feel ashamed to be a Cleveland fan.

Chris joins us in our gloom. She can't shake the memory of Red Right 88, especially tonight. Her dad was at the game; she and her sisters were home watching. They had friends over for the game. Just a bunch of Cleveland girls giddy over Brian Sipe and the Kardiac Kids—they've made posters and hung brown and orange crepe over the fireplace mantel. It's a little party.

Sipe tosses the interception, but hey—it's *still* a party. These are young teens, innocent, free of care. The Browns lost and that's sad, but they've got cookies and hot cocoa and a fire in the fireplace on a bitter-cold day. The Browns lost, but that's all right. Life will take the hurt away.

Then her dad walks in the door, blind drunk and half frozen, takes a look around, and loses his mind. He's bellowing the singsong Cleveland football chant—"*Here we go, Brow-nies, here we go*"—like he's back at the Stadium, and while he chants, he starts tearing down and crumpling all the posters and signs and crepe paper and throwing it into the fireplace while the girls scream in fear.

"Scared the hell out of us," she says now. "You would've thought that would've been it for me, but it just made me a crazier fan."

Cousin Jeff points down to the crowd behind the Cavs basket. There are two guys holding up a sign toward the press area. The sign reads "Scott Raab Is the Man."

What the fuck. It barely registers at that moment. It's way too weird. I'm at a Cleveland game and two guys are holding up a sign with my name on it. No way.

"You should go down there," says Chris.

I'm too embarrassed.

"You want me to go?" she asks.

Yes. Take my phone—get a picture of it, please. And tell them it means a lot to me.

JAMES SCORES 21 points in the third. He runs by the Cavs bench on almost every Heat possession, talking shit. The score after three quarters is 95–65.

The Cavs players sit there, stone-faced. Dan Gilbert never comes out for the second half.

No one in a Cavs uniform stands up to James. No one stands up for the team, the fans, the town. One assistant coach tells him to shut the fuck up, and that is the sum total of the Cavs' show of pride and strength and loyalty to their fans. No one fouls LeBron hard; they all but wave as he goes by.

James sits for the entire fourth quarter; he has 38 points in 30 minutes, 8 assists, and zero turnovers. It is by far his best game of the young season—and the Heat's. Mo Williams, who called this game "our Super Bowl" and urged the fans to stay cool, scores 11 points on 2–8 shooting.

In the Cavs locker room, the players can barely look at one another. I can barely look at them.

Saying goodbye in the press room before I hit the road, I almost take a swing at a Miami writer who shook my hand and said, "I felt sorry for Cleveland tonight."

Spare us your pity, hack.

IT'S A LONG ride home, 450 miles, with plenty of time to think.

I don't have spirit enough to put on the radio and listen to the postgame shows. I don't know if I can even watch another NBA game. Fuck the Cavaliers. With LeBron, they turned themselves into a clown car driven backwards by an infant: The Finals in 2007, the conference finals in 2009, the semis in 2008 and 2010. Abandoned now, his old teammates genuflect before him. Not one player or coach on that team was man enough to step up while that asshole was bent over in front of the home bench, talking smack right in their faces. Nary an elbow or a shove in the back while he and his new chorus line humiliated them on the floor he once bestrode, in presumptive glory.

That I will not forgive. The Cavaliers are dead to me.

• • • •

WHAT IS ALL this suffering worth? To ask, "Why, Lord?" while I roast alive another seven months on the spit of David Stern's indifference? Not enough, to witness LeBron waltz into the Q and disembowel my town; not enough to curse myself for caring; not enough to have already spent so much of my life on this ridiculous mission? Why go on? Is the road ahead not clear? Is there any way the Heat won't win it all?

Dayenu. A thousand times: Dayenu.

I'M PAST CLEARFIELD, halfway home, when I recall the sign.

"Scott Raab Is the Man."

Good enough.

I am nobody's hero but my son's, and not his for much longer. I'm glad he'd rather play than watch. I see no trace of fan's insanity in him; I hope I never do. I don't want him to be a writer if he comes to it as I did, drowning and desperate. But I know another kid, back in Cleveland, fatherless, fat, and frightened, pissing into a Folger's can at his grandparents' house, living game to game because the games are all that make his life seem worth its suffering.

The sign, it's not silly to that kid. That sign is the greatest thing the fat kid has ever seen. The fat kid, I'm starting to like him a little bit. From now on, the fat kid's riding up front, here with me.

CHAPTER THIRTEEN

FRANZ KAFKA BOBBLEHEAD NIGHT

hat loss lingers like no other. The Heat leave Cleveland and win 18 of their next 19 games. Erik Spoelstra grows six inches. Dwyane Wade and LeBron James trade riffs like Clapton and Duane Allman. Miami's defense is as ferocious as its offense is fluid. They began December with a record of 10–8; they finish 25–9, winning 10 of 10 road games, allowing 100 points exactly once. To a man, coach and player alike, they say it was the game against the Cavaliers that truly made them a team.

The Cavs, on the other hand, leave Cleveland without bothering to pack the testicles Miami stomped. They fly first to Minneapolis, where they yield 73 points in the first half and lose by 34 to the 4–15 Timberwolves. Then Detroit, where they lay down for the Pistons, another league doormat. Then Philly, a 20-point loss. Then home, for more of the same. The Cavs began December 7–10; they finish 8–24.

Dayenu. Most nights, they aren't playing to win; they play because the bus dropped them off at the arena. It's no longer possible to defend against the claim that James had to leave if he hoped to ever win a championship. Never mind that the Cavs have changed coaches and systems and several players, that they were built to complement a single unstoppable force, and that many so-called experts picked them to win it all the past two years. After their fainting spell on December 2, they have taken to bed with the vapors. Night after night, Byron Scott stands on the sideline, arms crossed, waiting for his team to show up. The players, pleased to draw their paychecks, wait with him.

THE HEAT ARE coming to New York to face the Knicks on December 17, and I have a lunch interview on the Upper West Side with Chris Rock three days before the game. When he says he'll be in Saint Martin with his family, I ask if I can have his seat.

"I already gave it up," he says.

I'm writing a book about LeBron.

"I don't even see what the big story is. The owner's an idiot. I was at a Lakers game—it was on TNT, and they asked me about LeBron. I said, 'They should trade him.' On national television."

We thought he was coming back.

"You could've got any player, literally any player outside of Kevin Durant and Dwight Howard. You could've got any two or three players you liked. The day the season was over, they asked me again, 'Where's LeBron going, what's going to happen?' I said, 'Well, if he's going to Cleveland, you will know within twenty-four hours, but if Pat Riley gets him in a room, it's *all over*.'"

We thought he was coming back.

"*Why* would you think he's coming back? People move from Cleveland to Miami every fucking day. They don't move from Miami to Cleveland."

You're killing me, man. Killing me.

"It's *Cleveland*, man. And I'm not disparaging Cleveland."

Yeah. You are.

"Look, if I'm twenty-five—even though he's got a baby mama, he's not married. Where the fuck is he going to go? Who didn't see this guy going to Miami?"

We didn't see him going to Miami.

"Dude, they're on the fucking beach right now. In fucking sandals."

He's got a big LOYALTY tattoo.

"Loyalty to *friends*. And all his friends are there. He's surrounded by six twenty-five-year-old black guys—where do you think they want to be? In Miami."

MY TICKET GUY, Joe D., loathes LeBron. Joe was so sure LeBron was coming to the Knicks that he loaded up on season tickets, certain he'd cash in. When I tell Joe I'm from Cleveland, he throws in a food voucher.

"I never thought I'd meet somebody who hates that dick more than I do," says Joe.

Madison Square Garden is full of haters. Somehow,

nobody has warned New York City not to give itself a black eye. "Fuck you, LeBron" shouts punctuate the National Anthem, and the crowd lets loose each time he touches the ball. The Knicks fight hard for a half, and then the Heat defense throttles the life out of Amar'e Stoudemire and the crowd; New York loses by 22 points, and James posts a triple-double.

"Best basketball venue in the world," he says afterward. "The fans here are great."

When I get home, Lisa and Judah are asleep. The dog and I watch the replay of the Cavs loss to Indiana earlier. The Pacers are up by only 5 at halftime, and the Cavs look like they've chosen to play hard tonight.

Don't spoil the ending, I tell the dog. For all I know, he watched it while I was at the Garden.

The Cavs lose by 9—their tenth loss in a row.

THE KNICKS FLY to Cleveland after the Heat game, and the Cavaliers beat them in overtime the next night to end the 10-game skid. They then celebrate by losing their next 26 games, the longest losing streak in NBA history.

Dan Gilbert is laying low. He's paying a Cleveland law firm to try to build a tampering case against Count Riley and the Heat. On a road trip to Orlando and Miami early last season, James was peppered with questions after Dwyane Wade told reporters that he and LeBron had talked about joining forces; James responded by saying that he'd no longer answer any questions about free agency. The next night, after the Cavs beat the Heat, James announced that he had decided to change his number from 6 to 23, explaining that Michael Jordan was of such unique importance to the NBA that no other player should ever wear his number.

"I'm starting a petition, and I've got to get everyone in the NBA to sign it," James said. "Now, if I'm not going to wear number 23, then nobody else should be able to wear it."

It was no secret, of course, that younger LeBron chose 23 to honor Jordan. Nor that the only team in the NBA to have retired 23 in tribute to MJ was the Heat. Nor that Michael himself was at the Cavs-Heat game that night, sitting courtside with Patula.

The whole thing amounted to no more than one day's news in a November already forgotten, and no big deal; LeBron had worn 6 in the Olympics, and had spoken idly about changing numbers in the past. Now it's at the heart of a hypothetical case that also involves a so-called secret meeting last June, where James, Wade, and Bosh agreed to sign with the Heat, weeks before the official opening of free agency.

I don't know if Dan Gilbert is any more serious about this than James was about his 23 petition; serious or not, he has no prayer. The NBA wouldn't investigate a tampering charge involving LeBron if Gilbert handed David

Stern a time-stamped video of Pat Riley sinking his fangs into LeBron's neck.

Forget it, Dan—it's Cleveland, where the quest for justice ends at the city limits and every night is Franz Kafka Bobblehead Night: every second fan gets a doll and the rest get punched in the nuts.

THE HEAT LEAVE the Garden after LeBron's triple-double on December 17 and win 10 of their next 11, highlighted by a Christmas Day beatdown of the Lakers in LA, with LeBron putting up yet another triple-double.

As it becomes clear just how good Miami is, an awful certainty descends. The Heat *will* win it all; LeBron James *will* get his ring. With the certainty comes the sadness of surrender: seven seasons in Cleveland, zero titles. It is finished.

Only then does my anger give way to despair. It always does. It always has. When my first wife was in residency and I was in the process of dynamiting our marriage, I went to get my diagnosis of bipolar. Given the family history and the life I'd led, I had no doubt. So I took my lithium, chasing it with bourbon and hydroponic bud, and next thing I knew I was living alone with the mastiff and the pistol-grip Mossberg 12-gauge in the old one-room schoolhouse an hour outside of Philly.

I was . . . troubled. Baseball was on strike, just when

the Indians were getting good. The dog was more than I could handle. Lisa was more than I could handle. The job was more than I could handle. I wasn't turning in my drafts. I was dodging phone calls from my editor.

The only TV channel I could get was NBC, and *Friends* had just debuted, and I knew it would be huge—and *Friends* was the last straw: I couldn't live on a planet where *Friends* was a smash.

Fetus me no fetuses: I might've been able to handle *Friends* if not for the dead baby. Not both, though. I don't believe that I was sober one waking moment in the fall and early winter of 1994. The dead baby was dead. Never spoke a word. The Mossberg wouldn't shut up.

The gun and I were going to tune in on Thursday at 8:30 for a very special episode of *Friends*. At some point that week, I went to see a guy in Philly, some psychologist. The shrink who wrote my lithium scrips had asked me what other drugs I was using—I'm sure now that she meant prescribed drugs—and when I finished my list, she said, *This guy. Go see this guy.*

Arnie. Arnold B. Jensky. Brawny Jew, old school Brooklyn accent, blue-collar to the core—he's missing the tips of two fingers and half of another that got chopped when he was installing roof vents in Union City, New Jersey—and no bullshit. He knows why I'm here, even if I'm not yet sure.

He asks, I tell him.

How often do I drink and drug?

Every day.

How many times a day?

All day.

How many years?

Twenty. Twenty-five. I took a couple of years off a few years ago, before I moved to Philly.

The lithium?

I don't feel the lithium. When I remember to take it.

We talk about my job, what's left of it. We talk about the dog. I don't mention the shotgun or dead baby.

What kind of dog?

Neapolitan mastiff.

Arnie laughs.

"Cowboys don't ride no ponies," he says.

I have no idea what he means, but I like him. I have a condescending fondness for psychotherapists, which goes with my belief, based on long experience, that they're generally weird and ineffectual. This guy is different. This guy is for real.

"I'd like to work with you," Arnie says. " But it'd be a waste of time unless you stop drinking and getting high."

Just like that?

"Yeah. Just like that."

Hey, I'm not sure I'm ready for that.

"Me neither," he says. "You're way down the road."

Whoa. I'm not *that* crazy.

"Really," Arnie says. "Then you tell me what your life would look like right now if you *were* that crazy."

He had me there.

"I'm willing to work with you. But you've got to be willing to give it up. I can't help you otherwise. No one can."

There are all kinds of ways to save somebody's life. That's how Arnie Jensky saved mine.

EARLY IN THE Cavs' big streak, I hit the road to Cleveland with Lisa and Judah; it's the week between Christmas and New Year's, so the boy is on break. It'll be good for my mother to see him—he has nothing on his nose but freckles—and I'll be able to check the Cavs' pulse.

"Let me know if you find one," a beat writer says at practice. "These guys laugh in the locker room after they lose. A lot of 'em are just happy to get the check."

Byron Scott hasn't yet ruled out the playoffs.

"We still got fifty games left, fifty-two. I think my job now is to be a little more harsh, holding them accountable."

The next night, the wife and son and I watch the Cavs take a comfy 15-point loss to the Magic. The full house is in fine fettle as the home team hangs tough for three quarters, but when Orlando pours it on in the fourth quarter the Cavs roll over and play dead.

Three nights later, on New Year's Eve, my mother

joins us for dinner. It's only 5:30 p.m. and she asks our waiter if the early-bird special is available on the holiday.

I'm buying, I tell her. Order whatever you want.

"I want the early-bird," she says.

You're embarrassing me.

"Shush."

Don't *shush* me, Ma.

Last night LeBron celebrated his twenty-sixth birthday with a party in Miami. The cake was over six feet tall, with a crown made of fondant. I saw photos online of him with his cake. Gloria and Savannah, his girlfriend, flew down from Ohio and they posed with the cake, too.

I'm thinking, next birthday I'll get me a big-ass cake. Instead of a fondant crown, I'll have a Mogen David made of kichel on top; instead of a huge "LJ" in gold flake, my cake will say, "Don't *Shush* Me, Ma." I'm up in the air about inviting Lucille, though. By then, the thing on my nose might have its own zip code.

THE CAVS LOSING streak sits at 20 when I head back to Miami at the end of January. Times are tough in Cleveland. Cousin Jeff, unwilling to bear the pain of watching the Cavs, is selling his seats at the Q game by game. For Friday night, against the Bucks, the high bid for a $95 face-value ticket is $1.49; he takes it. The Browns' season ends with home losses to archrivals Baltimore and Pittsburgh in front of thousands of empty seats and the ritual axing of the head coach.

The Heat are 33–14; their only rough patch since 12/2 follows immediately after the Cavs meet the Lakers on January 11 and suffer the worst thrashing in the team's history. In the first half, the Cavaliers explode for 25 points, total. Thanks to a blistering second half, they finish strong and lose 112–57.

"Karma is a bitch," James tweets during the fourth quarter of the Cavs' loss. "It's not good to wish bad on anybody. God sees everything!"

Not always, to be sure, but apparently tonight. The Heat lose their next game, to the Clippers, James rolls his ankle, and Miami proceeds to drop five of its next six games.

The Cavs are here to play the Heat on Monday, January 31, but I've arrived Saturday to see the world-famous Cleveland Orchestra, which began an annual winter residency in Miami in 2007. Despite harboring Gloria Estefan, this cultural sinkhole has no philharmonic of its own.

The concert features *Ein Heldenleben* ("A Hero's Life"), Richard Strauss's tone poem, which is explicated in two single-spaced pages in the program in a font so small I can't make it out.

"There is no need for a program," Strauss once noted. "It is enough to know there is a hero fighting his enemies." Suits me fine: I'm thrilled just to sit and enjoy a performance unmarred every few minutes by a mascot firing T-shirts into the cheap seats. And I'm proud, too: Cleveland fans have been rooting for the orchestra's laundry since 1918.

THE HIGHLIGHT OF the Cavs-Heat game comes late in the first quarter, when hip-hop impresarios P Diddy and Rick Ross make their way to their courtside seats across from the Heat bench. I'm only a couple of rows off the court—hot as the Heat are, Miami doesn't care, and it's easy to find great seats below face value—a few seats closer to the aisle than Gloria and Savannah, who've also made the trip. Pat Riley's one section over, with his wife of many centuries, Mrs. Pat Riley.

The game itself is the usual scrimmage. Wade's hotter than LeBron and goes for 34 points; James settles for 24 and 8 dimes. At no point does either squad look overly concerned about the outcome. The final is 117–90, and I'm heading for a pulled-pork omelet at Big Pink.

THE NEXT MORNING, I drive to Divine Delicacies, the shop that made LeBron's birthday cake. It looks like any other strip-mall bakery, but the display case is full of celebrity-cake photos, including LeBron's. Pride of place, though, goes to Dwyane Wade.

"We've done two cakes for Dwyane this year," says Laura, who manages the joint. "His favorite flavor is vanilla with the lemon frosting."

What about LeBron? What's his favorite?

"LeBron had five different flavors—red velvet, Godiva chocolate, guava cream cheese, the marble, and vanilla rum."

Laura excuses herself and comes back with an oval tray holding samples of each of LeBron's frostings.

They're all delicious, but I've got to go with the guava cream cheese, sweet and tart.

"I don't think he ever had a cake like that," Laura says. "I was at the party, and when he got there, he started dancing—then right away he got his phone and he took a picture of the cake.

Let me try that red velvet again.

"You said you're writing a book about him."

Mmmmf.

"Good or bad?"

Both, I lie. Some of both. More bad, I guess. I'm from Cleveland.

"What that owner did was out of line," she says. "He doesn't own him. He served him for so many years—he gave the city a lot of fame."

I'd like to set her straight—truly I would—but first I want to polish off the vanilla rum.

. . .

THAT NIGHT—I'm flying home in the morning—I realize how much I like Miami. Not the weather, which I find too hot and humid even in January, but the *feel* of it—easygoing, exotic, eager to please. You could almost say *sensual*. Almost.

I want to avoid that word because I mistrust it. It is animal, dangerous, unbounded. In a moral universe, sensuality feels like a threat. It must be distilled, channeled, sublimated into the abstract: fine art, music, poetry, even sport. Handjobs, of course. And compulsive eating.

I treat myself to sushi on Collins Avenue. The place is almost empty, so I set up my computer at a four-top and dig in. Excellent. So fine that when I'm done, I order a toro ceviche. I'm not hungry; I just don't want the meal to end.

When the ceviche is gone, I notice a blonde walking back and forth in front of my table, looking at me. Smiling.

This is not where I'd expect to find a hooker on a Thursday night at ten o'clock. But I can think of no other explanation as she comes and goes. I've lost a little weight, yeah. I've cut my hair and shaved my beard. And all that makes me is a fat old man with a laptop, a belly full of raw fish and rice, and a wife and son in New Jersey.

"Can I sit down?" she says.

I nod. She's blurry drunk. Late twenties, early thirties. High mileage.

She reaches across the table and rubs her hand along my arm.

You've mistaken me for someone else, I say. I'm not in the market.

"I'm not a prostitute," she says.

Then why are you sitting here?

"You seem like a nice man."

I am a nice man. I have a nice wife and a nice son and a nice dog. His name is Pip.

She seems near tears.

"I just wanted to talk to you," she says.

Three marriages. The first two husbands liked to smack her around. The last turned out to be gay. No kids. No college. No home. She's bunking a few blocks away at a hostel, waiting for a friend to wire money. She'll need to look for work next week if the money doesn't come. Her name is Donelle.

She's rubbing my arm again.

I have to go, I say, closing the laptop. I have an early flight tomorrow.

She doesn't move until I stand up, grab my briefcase, and start to leave. She stands and blocks my path. Puts her hand on my arm and bends her face toward me. She wants a kiss.

I kiss her on her cheek, and she moves her parted lips to mine.

No.

That's the word I want, and want to avoid: *no.*

No.

I give my son plenty of advice. I was forty-seven when he was born, and any insurance actuary can confirm how few sixty-year-old, 300-plus-pound men make it to seventy, so I like to keep it pithy. And even though he'll always be my child, he's already becoming the man he'll grow up to be, and there are things he needs to know.

Always bring a handkerchief.

Assume nothing in this world but my love for you.

Don't mistake fear for cowardice. Don't *ever* panic. Trust yourself and you'll figure it out.

Righty-tighty, which I learned from a goy.

Most important of all: say no.

No is the most powerful word in the language, I tell him. Especially for the son of a drunk. Especially then.

Donelle hears the no. The no cuts the air clean through.

I'm still a nice man. Nicer than I've ever been.

CHAPTER FOURTEEN

A STRANGE
WHITE MAN
AT
CENTER COURT

After I get back home, Judah and I watch LeBron go off for 51 points against Orlando. He makes his first 11 shots, and when the Magic whittle a 23-point deficit to 3 near game's end, James hits a 3-pointer and a pair of free throws to nail down a 4-point win.

"He's hard to hate when he plays like that," Judah says as we head upstairs.

I can manage it, kid. It's right in my wheelhouse. Hell, it's my sacred duty. I'm from Cleveland.

"You *are* Cleveland," he says.

EVERY NIGHT, UNLESS I'm on the road, I wait while my son flosses and brushes his teeth. Then he lies down and we talk. My father was a salesman on the road when I was younger than Judah is now, and I can remember his voice on the phone. I remember his smell when we'd wrestle: Old Spice and sweat. I don't know what my boy will remember. I'm not sure it matters. What matters is this moment between the end of his day and my trek up to the third floor to write, when we lay together and he says, "Tell me a story."

I got no stories, kid.

"You've got stories."

You know all my stories already.

"I *know* that's not true."

You know all the stories I want you to know. How about a joke?

"Okay."

You know the one about the cross-eyed schoolteacher?

"No."

She couldn't control her pupils.

He snorts. "Tell me another," he says.

One more. Then I have to get to work.

"Okay."

Old man gets knocked down by a car. The driver stops and gets out, scared to death. The old man's lying there, conscious and groaning. The driver calls 911 and tells the old man not to worry—an ambulance is on the way. He takes off his jacket, folds it up, puts it under the old man's head, and asks the old man if he's comfortable.

The old man looks up at him and says, "I make a living."

"I don't get it," Judah says.

You will. Now go to sleep, sweetheart.

When he becomes a father, *kinehora*, he'll know that the jokes and stories don't matter. What matters are these moments. Fifty years later, I remember my father's smell, but I had just turned ten when my mother left Los Angeles for Cleveland with my brothers and me, and after that there were no moments.

I could lie beside my son all night, just listening to

him breathe. I head up to the office, thinking about LeBron. If I grew up feeling fatherless, hurt, and angry, how much worse it must have been for him. He had no one to miss. No smell. Nothing.

Now he's living in Miami, and his six-year-old and three-year-old sons are in Ohio and go weeks at a time without seeing him. I wonder what it is that he thinks echoes in eternity? Triple-doubles?

ON FEBRUARY 11, his boys are courtside in Detroit to see him play against the Pistons when a front-row fan inquires loudly of James whether Gloria is heading to Boston to spend Valentine's Day with Delonte.

James walks over.

"What did you say to me?"

"I said, 'Is your mom going to Boston for Valentine's Day?'"

"Say whatever you want to say to me," James tells him. "Just don't get disrespectful."

The fan shuts up. A security guard warns him against any further badinage. LeBron is praised far and wide for defending his sons against a heckler so nasty as to insult their grandmother. But did the heckler know those were his sons? Does anyone but me wonder why—since he has been reviled by Pistons fans his entire career, and since the Palace of Auburn Hills is notorious for its nastiness—LeBron thought it was a good idea for his little boys to attend a Friday night game there?

The Heat win, of course, 106–92; their record now stands at 39–14.

That same night, the Cavaliers beat the Los Angeles Clippers in overtime, ending their losing streak after 26 games and bringing their own record to a gaudy 9–45. Since playing the Heat on 12/2, they're 2–34.

WORD COMES THAT very week from California: Sandy Raab is in the loony bin. The precipitating event— the sudden departure of the Filipina who'd followed the Gypsy into and out of his bed and his heart—plunged him into a depression no less profound nor painful for all its familiarity.

I knew he was back in the hole when I returned from Miami and heard him on my voice mail, barely able to speak. I call him back and he manages to tell me that she done left him and he's thinking of killing himself.

I ask about his meds and he starts a song-and-dance about how the shrink prescribed another antidepressant to combat this latest swing, but my father hasn't gone out to get the pills yet.

"What's the use?" he says.

That's not a question; that's depression. The only question is, Why aren't you following your doctor's orders?

"I'm sorry I called," he says.

Me, too. I'm in New Jersey. What do you expect me to do from here? Call Michael.

Michael's my half brother. He lives in Burbank. When my mother took us back to Cleveland, my father married the woman he was having an affair with, and Michael is their progeny. I know from talking to Michael that he confiscated Sandy's .38 Police Special after the Gypsy left and the old man started waxing suicidal. Let Michael deal with this, too.

Michael lets his wife handle it, and when Sandy calls and tells Michael's wife he feels like killing himself, she takes him at his word, phones 911, and they give Sanford a lift to the mental health ward at Northridge Hospital.

I'm heading to Boston, where the Celtics kindly credential me for their game against the Heat on 2/13. The Celtics have whipped Miami both times they've played this season, and the Heat, riding an 8-game win streak, try to whistle past the graveyard—this game isn't a test, they say, isn't make-or-break, isn't a big deal. But the teams are essentially tied for the best record in the East, and the Heat will have to beat Boston to reach the Finals. The Celtics are down to eight healthy players today. It is indeed a test, and the whole league knows it.

Especially the Heat. As the Celtics pull away in the third quarter, Dwyane Wade hammers Kevin Garnett with an elbow in the back, drawing a flagrant foul. As the officials huddle to discuss the call, Boston's Rajon Rondo wanders over to where the Heat are gathered around Spoelstra. Rondo leans in to listen, unnoticed until James nudges him away. Rondo eases himself right back to where he was when James nudged him. LeBron just glares; finally, the Celtics' Ray Allen comes and leads Rondo away.

The subtext of Rondo's clowning seems clear enough. Disrespecting the Heat is a tactic, part of beating them. The Celtics lead by 13 going into the fourth, but the Heat, led by LeBron, come back. With 19 seconds left, James misses a free throw that would've tied the game. With 6 seconds left and Miami down 3, James passes the ball to Mike Miller, a bargain-basement free agent who has missed 3 of 4 shots today, all from long range. He's wide open, but Miller bricks the 3-pointer and Miami loses, 85–82.

That same day, in Cleveland, the Cavs' one-game winning streak dies when the Washington Wizards, 0–25 on the road so far this season, build a 22-point halftime lead and coast to a 115–100 victory.

"I'm still trying to figure them out," Byron Scott says of his eunuch legion. "Because to me, that was ridiculous."

I don't know, Coach. It's no more ridiculous than paying you $4 million to stand on the sideline with your arms crossed and your mustaches twitching with disdain.

Aren't you supposed to be *motivating* these guys somehow? Or does that cost extra?

As for the Heat, with two-thirds of the season played, with the game on the line against the Celtics, with no time left on the clock, and with LeBron James, Dwyane Wade, and Chris Bosh on the floor, the guy taking the final shot is Mike Miller.

Fifteen hundred miles away in Miami, Pat Riley sniffs the wind and winces. Garlic.

SANDY GOES FROM the psych ward to an assisted-living apartment in the Valley.

"I feel abandoned," he says on the phone.

You're not abandoned. You're on the phone with me.

"I wish you were out here," he says.

No. I'm right where I belong.

Three thousand miles away, my father hears the no.

"I know that," he says.

ON FEBRUARY 24 a miracle: Mo Williams shipped to the Los Angeles Clippers for Baron Davis and a first-round draft choice. It is nothing short of a complete reversal of the Dayenu Principle. Ridding the Cavs of Mo by any means is good enough. Baron Davis, despite his flaws—he's aging, fat, oft-injured, and cranky—is a nice fit. He's an alpha dog. He has played, not always happily, for Byron Scott; and—when he's feeling it—B Dizzle has that same canine hunger that Shaq prized in Delonte.

Plus a number-one? *Plus?* From the Clippers, no less, as poorly run as any franchise in all of pro sports. It means that the Cavs are likely to have two lottery picks in the NBA draft this summer—their own and the hapless Clippers'.

And—praise Jesus—I never have to watch Mo Williams in a Cavalier uniform ever again.

Trust me, though, I am not blind to the pathos here. My life as a Cleveland fan has come to this: the Cavs, 44–14 a year ago, are 10–47; Miami is 42–16; LeBron is playoff-bound; and I'm shouting hosannas. No Mo.

WITH BARON DAVIS feeling it, the Cavs play like an NBA team. Not a good NBA team, but that's okay; they no longer look like a team with no hope of winning or interest in trying. Even Byron Scott gets into the spirit, occasionally uncrossing his arms. He and Baron are at peace. With Davis leading the pack, the Cavs bear little resemblance to the curs who played dead on 12/2.

The news out of Florida is heartening, if strange: the Heat have been reduced to tears. After a last-second one-point home loss to the Bulls on March 6—

the Heat's fourth straight loss, after James and Wade both miss last-second shots—Spoelstra tells reporters, "There are a couple guys crying in the locker room right now."

Wade bitches about wanting the ball in the fourth quarter. LeBron promises his teammates, "I'm not going to continue to fail late in the games." Bosh, the Heat's Eva Perón, captures the aching that follows "when you put your heart and your soul, your blood, your sweat, your tears into something, and you want something so bad and it just slips from you."

Two days later, with the mocking laughter still ringing around the NBA, Spoelstra accuses the media of sensationalism and says his boys weren't crying after all.

"I saw glossy eyes, but that's about it," he says.

The Heat have now gone more than a month without beating a team with a winning record. Their two main Eastern Conference rivals, the Bulls and Celtics, are a combined 6–0 against Miami. Riley's us-against-the-world approach has dissolved like the mascara on Chris Bosh's avian cheek as the team, its fans, and the Miami media commence moping without shame about feeling hated.

"The world is better now because the Heat is losing," Wade pouts.

To which Stan Van Gundy, the current Orlando Magic—and former Miami Heat—head coach, speaking on behalf of a weary but proud nation, replies, "If you don't want the scrutiny, don't hold a championship celebration before you've even practiced together."

THE CAVALIERS WON'T be printing playoff tickets anytime soon. Even with two lottery picks, they may not make the playoffs again for years. Before LeBron, the Cavs made the playoffs only 13 times in their 35 years of existence. They would have to win their next 250 games to even their all-time won-loss record.

The Browns rose from the dead in 1999, their rights sold by the NFL to Al Lerner, a billionaire who owned a slice of the old franchise and also introduced fellow Brooklyn-born Jew Art Modell to the Baltimore money men who financed Modell's theft of the team; Modell signed the papers that finalized that shabby heist on Lerner's private jet.

Al Lerner had chutzpah enough to call his bid for the New Browns "an act of conscience"; Fate rewarded him with brain cancer. Al died on the fourth anniversary of his acquisition of the team, leaving his son, Randy, in charge. The New Browns have a 12-year won-loss record of 64–128, with two winning seasons and one playoff game.

The Indians were purchased in 2000 by one of the failed bidders for the New Browns, Cleveland native Larry Dolan, a member of the Irish nincompoop clan that has so successfully run the New York Knicks into the ground. Larry has held his own by snuffing an entire fanbase. Ten years ago, the Tribe's streak of sold-out games ended at 455. Last season, the team ranked dead last in MLB attendance.

When I was born, Cleveland was America's seventh-largest city; now it ranks forty-third, and falling fast: the town lost 17 percent of its population between 2000 and 2010, and dropped below 400,000 for the first time in a century. Sometimes, especially for an expat, the mere existence of the Cavs, Browns, and Indians seems like all that keeps Cleveland from slipping into darkness forever.

And sometimes, especially this season, it feels like there is no Promised Land, only sand, like all hope is mirage and all memory a dream, like the Cleveland living in my heart and soul will die along with me.

Lord, I'm tired. Haven't I paid dues enough? Hasn't *Cleveland*? I'm not looking to cut a deal. I don't need another Yahwevian covenant, not when the last one cost a chunk of my penis *and* my son's, and for what? All I ask for is the strength to go on and finish the job, and that You keep half an eye on my wife and son. And maybe a shred of *rachmones* for Cleveland fans. Did I say a shred? I meant to say a scintilla. Let's start with a scintilla. Amen.

· · ·

I'M HEADED TO Cleveland one last time this season, for the return of the return of the Whore of Akron on March 29. Right now it's Sunday night, the twenty-seventh, and I've timed the drive so that I'm in the car on I-80 arrowing through Pennsylvania in time to hear Joe Tait call the Cavs-Hawks game tonight.

Tait began calling Cavs games in 1970, during their first season. He was thirty-three years old then, and it was his first big-time gig; the Cavs rookie coach, Bill Fitch, knew Tait from his student-radio days at Monmouth College in Illinois, where Fitch had coached basketball. Joe was Midwest-born and bred and sounded it, and his voice had a deadpan edge that perfectly suited a 15-win NBA expansion team. In the early '80s, the Cavs' radio rights went to a rival station for a year—Tait spent that season calling Nets games—but otherwise, Joe Tait has been the one and only voice of a team whose face was often ghastly to behold.

Hoping to call a Cavs championship before he retired, Joe hung on longer than he wanted to, and given his girth and the grueling travel that goes with the job, longer than he should have. Just before the regular season began, he came down with pneumonia, which led to blood clots in his lungs and, in January, double-bypass surgery.

Joe swore before he went under the knife that he'd come back to finish the year—his final year, at age seventy-three—and so he has, for the Cavs' last five home games, starting tonight.

I'm on I-80's last Pennsylvania leg, between Lamar and Sharon, when Joe signs on.

"It's basketball time at the Q," he says, same as ever.

No, I'm not crying. If my eyes are a little glossy, it's because I can still hear him calling the end of Game 7 against the Bullets during the Miracle of Richfield 35 years ago—and because that game turned out to be Joe Tait's championship.

THE DAY BEFORE the Heat game, I finally get back inside the owner's vault across from the Cavs' locker room with Dan Gilbert, who's trying to explain why he left his courtside seats at halftime on 12/2 and never came back.

"I was literally afraid of going out on that court," says Dan. "I knew what the asshole was doing, and I didn't want to—" and he stops.

"Sometimes I can lose my—" stop. I can see the red beginning to rise.

"He was *taunting*. He was loving every second of it. I wouldn't have physically gone after him, but I would have probably said and done some things that I would have regretted. So I didn't come out."

Your players came out. They came out, smiled pretty, and spread wide their cheeks.

"I guess it just wasn't a thought that entered our minds, that maybe these guys—look, some of them might've been Cavaliers for a few years, but they're not from Cleveland—they weren't born and raised here. He was a co-worker of theirs. We should've reminded 'em. If we'd said, 'Look, you need to understand how serious this is,' I think our players would've listened. I blame us more than them. I kick myself in the ass on that one. That'll always haunt me, because I think it was the beginning of the end of our season."

Gilbert's biggest regret, though, is losing all leverage when James committed for only three years in 2007 instead of signing a longer extension.

"When he said, 'I'm signing for three years,' we should've had the balls to say, 'Shove it.' He wouldn't have left. He wasn't prepared and ready to leave. We should've said, 'Fuck you. Go. Let's see it.'"

The fans would've been screaming for your blood, not his.

"I would've gone to the fans and explained it. How much we love LeBron, and how we're doing all we can to build a team around him to bring Cleveland a championship, and not just one. But LeBron has to step up, too. He has to commit long-term or it won't work. And if he's *not* willing to do that, I can't have one player hold the organization hostage. If he won't sign a long-term deal, I have to try and trade him for players who really want to be here."

I don't know, Dan. All I know is that the fans are the ones who always wind up suffering. That's just how it is in Cleveland.

"The Cleveland fan is the most undertold story in history," Gilbert says. "It's the best sports town in the world. I had a bunch of friends go to Miami for somebody's fiftieth birthday party, and they came back and said, 'How does he even go there? They don't give a shit about sports.'"

THAT NIGHT I take a psychiatrist to dinner, Dr. Richard Friedell. Rich was at the Browns title game in 1964, but he seems unburdened by a sense of deep frustration about Cleveland sports or rage over LeBron's departure.

"I don't care about the ring," he says. "I care about my team."

Well and good, but I myself can't help but feel a championship would make a profound and positive difference to Cleveland's collective psyche.

"The ring, the ring, the ring, the ring. Enough with this stuff."

But so many decades of failure. So much hope, dashed. So many dreams, dead. And then *this* guy comes along, and he's the best player in the league—and he's *from* here.

The good doctor is admiring his glass of red. He is beefy, florid, and full of irony.

"My wife was very fond of him," he says. "Who knows at what depth of personal fantasy?"

That's not what I'm talking about. I'm talking about

a lifetime of sports defeat and despair, culminating in a single act of treachery. I'm talking about the rage engendered by suffering decade after decade after decade with no release.

"Another reason for legalizing prostitution," says Dr. Friedell.

I'M DRIVING DOWN Lee Road to get my Game Day haircut Tuesday morning when Friedell calls. His friend Howard Edelstein has an extra ticket for the Cavs game and would be honored if I'd join him and his son, Brian.

I call Howard, who turns out to be an original Cavs season-ticket holder; his seats are in the third row behind the visitors' bench. I tell him that he might not want me sitting with him; if I'm not in the press box, I'm going to get loud.

Not a problem, says Howard.

Excellent.

Lee Road heading north is full of memories. Uncle Manny owned a TV repair shop in Maple Heights—long gone, like Manny, who took his flatulence to Florida in the '90s and passed away there. Once I reach Cleveland Heights, I'm home.

Cedar and Lee was where the shoe store used to be. When I started working there in 1972, the first wave of blacks had moved to Cleveland Heights from the inner city and a lot of the white people began moving farther east. Now the surburb's population is evenly divided, more or less, but only in terms of overall numbers. Heights High, whose campus sprawls from one quadrant of the Cedar-Lee intersection, is three-quarters black now, and the town has lost more than a quarter of its population since 1970.

Lee Road is black. The barbershop, Center Court, is black. The barber, Dmitri Sumbry, is black. I'm white, and I know enough to know that a strange white man strolling into a black barber shop is indeed a *strange* white man. I know I'll be only three rows behind the Heat bench: and I want a message razored into my hair—something special from me to the Whore of Akron. So I've arranged my haircut in advance by getting in touch with the writer Jimi Izrael, whose own barber is Dmitri.

I want something else, too: I want to have a conversation with a black guy about my animus toward LeBron. Jesse Jackson and Maverick Carter and a few black voices in the media have weighed in on the role race played in the reaction to The Decision. Some claim it's a factor, some deny it—I'm not looking for antipathy or absolution: I just want to know what I don't know. I want to think about what I haven't thought of yet.

Jimi Izrael is a Cleveland guy, built like a nose tackle, with dreadlocks hanging down to his belt. Not a big sports fan, not a LeBron hater or lover: Jimi's a man of letters, a culture critic. Which must be why he's disappointed to see my shoes.

"You wore Crocs to a black barbershop? *Crocs?*"

I've got foot issues, man. They're swollen.

"In the barbershop, you have to come correct. Look around you: Nikes, Adidas, Jordans. Everyone rocks their fly sneakers at the barbershop—Crocs? Not so much."

Dmitri's quiet. He's pondering what to put on my head. Dmitri's a LeBron hater, so I've left it up to him. With my pale scalp and the whiteness of my hair, Dmitri has a lot of pondering to do.

"You know what?" Jimi says. "I think white Cleveland felt like they fed LeBron, clothed him, and never called him 'nigger' in so many words—so the least he could do is wear his body down for another few years carrying a team of glamour boys and flatfoots."

Come on, Jimi. He was treated like royalty here. Everything he wanted was his for the asking. He didn't even have to ask.

"Nah, man. This is *Cleveland*. All that 'mama' shit— your moms is loud and ghetto, you're a project kid, the bastard child of a troubled woman of easy virtue—that's some bullshit. Name a white athlete who ever had to put up with that kinda shit."

I thought the local media people went out of their way to avoid that stuff.

"You don't live here, man. That shit was on the air, daily for a minute—'*Who's LeBron's Daddy?*' I mean, leading the news. In a city leaking jobs and cops, the news is about LeBron's mama! Hate on me, my work—leave my moms out of it. Whenever you talk about a man's mother—a black man's mother—forget it. You've crossed a line. You've cut too deep."

It runs both ways, though, Jimi. Cleveland eats its own, no doubt. But home is home. And the kid wore that like he meant it. Like he *wanted* to be here.

"Listen: Freedom means something different, maybe something more, to black people. White folks look at LeBron and see a traitor who turned his back on his city. Black folks, even hardcore fans, see a black man making choices that suit him and his family—without hesitation or regret. Just like white folks do."

Jimi, we're talking about pro athletes. Loyalty is *always* an issue when a guy decides to leave. And this guy was one of us, or so we thought.

"Cleveland owed LeBron better. He owed us his best game, no more, no less. Hard to ask for more than that."

DMITRI DID HIS best, but you couldn't really see QUITNESS shaved around the sides and back of my head until he took a bloodred makeup pencil and filled in the letters.

To the Edelsteins' credit, they don't blink when we meet for a burger before the game. They don't blink when

I spend most of the first quarter standing and screaming at James whenever he gets close. There are plenty of fans doing the same, and never does LeBron so much as glance in my direction.

Halfway through the second quarter, my voice is gone, but my heart—my heart, it is singing. There will be no playoff game at the Q this season, but this is better, louder, and more joyful. The Cavaliers play hard—on one drive, James gets knocked on his ass; on another, his headband is torn off his head—and 20,562 Cleveland fans won't let them lose. Even as the Heat climb back into a tie from 23 points down, the Cavs rise up to smite them back down, and win by double digits for the first time all season, 102–90.

Thank you, Lord.

The loss drops Miami out of a tie with the Celtics for best record in the conference. For LeBron, it's one more empty triple-double. For the Cavs's players, it's redemption for 12/2. For the Cleveland fans, it's a victory that will glow forever. For me, it's a sweet ending to my last Cleveland trip of the season.

I'm so giddy that I invite my mother out for Thai food before I leave for home the next day.

"Is that stuff going to come out of your hair?"

Eventually. Most of it came off in the shower.

"You don't have any cuts on your scalp, do you?"

None that I'm aware of, no.

"You shouldn't get an infection."

I believe we've exhausted the subject, don't you?

"They're really going to call the book *The Whore of Akron*?"

Yep.

"Is that all right with *Esquire*?"

I hope so.

"Did you check with them?"

Don't worry about it. Worst-case scenario, I come back here and move in with you.

CHAPTER FIFTEEN

ENDGAME

In the end, the Heat finish the regular season with a worse record than LeBron's last two Cavs teams—58 wins total, only 11 more than Miami won last season. But they finish strong, winning 7 of their last 8, including their first and only victory against the Celtics in four tries this season. The only bump on the Heat's season-ending road comes six hours or so after their one loss, when Gloria James staggers out of the Fountainbleau Hotel at 4:45 a.m. and slaps the valet parking attendant for his failure to rustle up her car fast enough. The Miami Beach police book her for battery and disorderly intoxication and release her.

LeBron wasn't at the Fountainbleau.

"Tough game last night," he tells reporters after practice the next day. "I decided to get my rest."

I'm lucky by comparison. Lucille's most embarrassing habit is to claim that it's her birthday at a restaurant, hoping that the waitress will fetch her dessert on the house. I would not want to watch a surveillance video clip of my mother on TMZ, swinging her purse at the waitress when the cupcake fails to arrive, and falling on her ass.

PLAYOFF FEVER, MIAMI-STYLE: before each home game, the Heat place white slipcovers over the seats in the hope that TV viewers will say, "Wow, what's up with all those white slipcovers?" rather than, "Where the hell are all the so-called Heat fans?"

Far easier to mock the slipcovers than to contemplate the games themselves, and the pain of watching them. In the second round, against the once-mighty Celtics—too old, too slow, too hurt—LeBron is the hammer of doom, pounding Boston at the Garden for 35 points and 14 rebounds in a Game 4 overtime win, then, back in Miami, scoring the Heat's final 10 points in a game-ending 16–0 run that also closes out the series.

When the game ends, LeBron drops to one knee and bows his head. Then he rises from the floor, wet-eyed, and embraces Wade. I'm dry-eyed, watching on TV. It's May 11, a year to the day after James's last home game as a Cavalier—the worst game of his seven seasons in Cleveland, the worst home playoff loss in franchise history—when he wandered lonely as a cloud through Game 5 against these Celtics, when he cracked and broke and fell apart.

AT THE POSTGAME press conference, asked what he was feeling as he knelt, LeBron unlocks the wee jewel box of his soul to offer what most of the sports world will hear as a sincere apology for The Decision: "Everything went through my mind at that point—everything

I went through this summer, deciding to come down here to be part of this team. I knew how important team is. I knew deep down in my heart, as much as I loved my teammates back in Cleveland, as much as I loved home, I couldn't do it by myself. And all the backlash I got, I went through a lot, the way it panned out with the fans and family and friends back home. I apologize for the way it happened, but I knew that this opportunity was once in a lifetime."

Happy Anniversary! I made something special just for you: a half-assed apology, swaddled in self-pity and the certainty that I did the right thing. I'm sorry that my Cleveland teammates sucked ass. Sorry I turned seven seasons of your adoration, gratitude, and hope into an hour of public humiliation. My bad.

Golly, LeBron, thanks. In return, might I suggest that you kiss my hairy Jewish ass?

AFTER A GAME 1 shellacking, Miami dismantles the Bulls in four straight with a series of second-half comebacks. James shuts down Derrick Rose, the league MVP, leads Miami in points, rebounds, and assists, saves a child from drowning in the hotel pool in Chicago, performs an emergency tracheotomy on a choking Heat Index reporter, and cures cancer.

That's essentially the ESPN narrative now: All hail

King James. Demonized, LeBron stood tall. Last July they burned his jersey in Cleveland; now it's the best-selling jersey in the league. It's The Vindication. The Redemption.

Huzzah.

Don't mind me, boys. I'll get the lights and lock up the joint.

THE TIME HAS finally come to face the horror at the heart of my quest. I hold no hope of a reprieve nor doubt about the suffering to come. I have known it all along. I've seen it coming since the night of July 8. I've lived my whole life as a Cleveland fan so that I might bear witness to the truth of it.

The greatest athlete in the history of Cleveland sports was born in Akron and grew up to become a world champion.

In Miami.

WHAT'S LEFT FOR a Jew and a Cleveland fan to do? Keep alive the memory and spirit of December 27, 1964. Embrace the wisdom of Viktor Frankl, whose master-work, *Man's Search for Meaning*, Arnie Jensky thrust upon me. Frankl was a psychiatrist who'd survived three Nazi concentration camps, and learned to find value in existence under the worst imaginable conditions.

"The salvation of man is through love and in love," Frankl wrote. "I understood how a man who has nothing left in this world still may know bliss, be it only for a brief moment, in the contemplation of his beloved. In a position of utter desolation, when man cannot express himself in positive action, when his only achievement may consist in enduring his sufferings in the right way—an honorable way—in such a position man can, through loving contemplation of the image he carries of his beloved, achieve fulfillment."

What else? Maybe see if Lisa has a spare moment or two.

THERE IS NO joy in Cleveland. I can't help that any more than I can help feeling guilty about it. When it comes to the sufferings of Cleveland, I'm just a tourist now. I left a quarter century ago, and I've enjoyed the kind of run I never could've had as a writer in Cleveland, even if I'd lived a sober day there.

But when it comes to the suffering of Cleveland fanhood, I staked my claim twenty years before LeBron James was born, and never for a moment have I relinquished it. On that soil I'll stand until I die.

All I can do now is see the mission through.

. . .

WHEN I BECAME a father, in 1999, I found I could no longer tolerate books or movies about young children in peril, so let me make plain that my son, *kinehora*, is fine. But on Memorial Day, one day before Miami and Dallas met in Game 1 of the Finals, he fell ill. Vomiting, headache, and a higher fever—102.5—than he'd run in years.

We took him to the doctor Tuesday, on the morning of the first game. Nothing to worry about, the doctor said. A bug. It's going around. A day, a day and a half, he'll be fine.

I sat in the rocker as Judah hacked and sweated and slept on the couch, and watched the Heat defense grind the Mavericks to powder in the first game of the series. Miami won, 92–84, and though Dallas kept it close, at no point did they look good enough to win. The Heat were quicker, faster, stronger, and playing with zest and confidence—particularly LeBron, who, in the first Finals victory of his career, led Miami in scoring and added 9 rebounds and 5 assists.

Worse, Dirk Nowitzki, the Mavs' longtime hero, in his thirteenth season with Dallas and still searching for his first title—he, too, had been a free agent last July, but chose to stay—tore a tendon in the middle finger of his left, nonshooting hand late in the game.

Judah slept through the night. I couldn't rouse him enough to get him up to bed.

I don't like the cough. I don't like the phlegm. I don't like how hot he feels when I lay my hand on his forehead.

"Go on up," the dog says. "I'll watch him."

Thanks, but I'm not tired. I'm worried.

"I'd say scared."

JUDAH WAKES UP, still on the couch, at ten in the morning, Wednesday, 15 hours after he fell asleep. I'm still in the rocker.

How you feel, kid?

"Not so good."

How's the headache?

"Bad."

On a scale of one to ten?

"Seven."

At least his temperature is down—a little under a hundred. He doesn't want to eat; he's queasy, he says. The cough sounds about the same. But he's not himself. I don't know any other way to think about it. He came home sick on Monday afternoon from the Brooklyn Botanic Gardens, threw up in the driveway as soon as Lisa pulled in. That was a little more than 36 hours ago, and he's still not himself.

• • •

HE'S TIRED ALL day Wednesday, but he can eat—a bagel, some rice and chicken. A constant stream of water. Cough drops. Tylenol for the headache. Not a great day, but better. No doubt about it. Better.

He wakes up Thursday worse. As the day goes on, the fever's back up above 101. The cough is heavier. The headache comes back. Around five p.m., he eats a small bowl of rice and a few bites of chicken and falls asleep on the couch.

I'm thinking meningitis. I've been studying meningitis online for three nights now. Me and the dog, all night long.

The dog thinks viral, which would be much less dire.

I'm thinking bacterial, because of the season. Bacterial is a version of the nightmare that comes home from the hospital with your newborn and never stops recurring even as it becomes the thing on your sixty-year-old baby's nose.

"Don't tell Lisa," says the dog. "She's worried enough as it is."

Game 2 tips off after nine p.m. with the boy wasted on the couch, and now I can feel the sweep coming. The Heat go up 88–73 with 7:33 to play when Wade hits a 3 from the sideline near the Dallas bench. Wade feels all sweepy too: He stands there, holding his pose after the shot falls. LeBron runs over to him and rat-a-tats his chest. Together they shimmy while the Mavs glare in disgust.

"There's no way we're going out like this," the Mavs Jason Terry says to Nowitzki. They were both on the 2006 Dallas team that lost to the Heat in the Finals, a series filled with blown calls and controversy.

"I can't watch this," Lisa says. "I can't stand watching that asshole."

She means LeBron, of course. Lisa's on the couch with Judah's feet resting on her legs. We're going back to the doctor in the morning.

Go on up. Get some sleep. The boy's fine. I'll keep an eye on him. This game's over anyway.

Wrong! Wrong! Beautifully, wonderfully wrong! Slow, methodical, relentless, the Mavericks come back. Miami's not even running an offense anymore; they're playing hero ball, with Wade and LeBron firing 3-pointers and missing. They don't even have sense enough to run time off the clock before they bomb away, and Coach Spo seems helpless to stop them.

Nowitzki scores Dallas's last 9 points—he even left-hands a couple of layins—in a 22–5 run that ends the game and evens the series at a game apiece.

I go upstairs to tell Lisa that Dallas won.

"You're kidding me," she says.

Nope. It was unbelievable.

"How's the boy?"

The same.

• • •

WHEN LISA WAS pregnant with Judah, we decided we'd wait until she delivered the baby to find out what flavor she was carrying. Fine with me. I was going to be thrilled either way; of that, I had no doubt. But as the weeks and months rolled by, I more and more wanted to know. Just to know—that's what I thought. Just to know.

It got to the point that I decided to check the clipboard one day at the doctor's when she went to get dressed and he was out of the room. And when I saw that we were going to have a boy, I knew why I wanted to know: because I wanted a boy. This boy.

Here he is. On the couch. Sick. The answer to every question I ever had about the meaning of life, about why I'm still around, why I got sober, why even the worst day of my life now is better than any day I ever had before I met him.

I wasn't hoping for someone to play catch with. I wanted a son because I wanted someone to love me the way I loved my old man, and to give me the chance to do right by that love. Which turns out to be nothing more complicated than being there when he needs me.

But what I couldn't possibly have known is what comes to me now as I sit and watch him sleep. More than I need anyone or anything in the world, I need him.

Of all the mirrors in the world, he's the one whose reflection matters most.

NO MENINGITIS. Mycoplasma pneumonia—they used to call it "walking pneumonia"—is what the boy has, and a five-day course of antibiotics will knock it out.

You might say I'm relieved. You might say I'm over-joyed. You might say I'm overtired, too; I haven't slept more than an hour or two at a stretch all week.

More than anything, I'm grateful that the real suffering to come remains for now just that: the suffering to come.

I'm thankful to the God I don't believe in for any deferral of the real suffering that comes—soon or late but always—to every one of us.

The real suffering to come has nothing at all to do with sports.

THE SERIES MOVES to Dallas for Game 3, and the Heat win, 88–86, on a late shot by Princess Bosh, to go up 2 games to 1.

Since the NBA went to a 2-3-2 playoff format in 1985, the team winning the third game of a 1–1 series has gone on to win the series 11 of 11 times. But something else is happening: Something is cracking inside LeBron.

He comes out strong early, and then stops. Stops driving to the basket. Stops defending close to the basket. Stops rebounding, stops shooting.

I'm hardly the only one to see this. With a little over three minutes to play and the Mavs making a last-ditch run, Wade is screaming at James as both teams line up for a Dallas free-throw attempt.

Wade's screaming because James had the ball on the Heat's previous possession, and rather than trying to score, James had quickly dumped it off to Mario Chalmers, who was too closely guarded to do much but turn it over. It was a boneheaded pass, thrown by a player who didn't want the ball in his hands.

They're still on the floor, and Wade's screaming so loud that the announcers can hear it.

James turns his back and walks away, toward the Heat bench. Wade follows, still screaming. James has nowhere to go now, and turns sideways, scowling. LeBron says something, and Wade, his back to the camera, stomps away.

AFTER GAME 3, Gregg Doyel, a CBS sports columnist, asks LeBron why he's shrinking in the fourth quarter.

James advises Doyel to study the game film with an eye to his sturdy late-game defense.

"You'll ask me a better question tomorrow," LeBron tells Doyel.

Plenty of Doyel's sportswriter colleagues—"lumps of well-dressed clay," in Hunter S. Thompson's phrase—scorn him as a troll for his question. But Doyel's right: James has scored a total of 9 fourth-quarter points in the series' first 3 games.

THE GERMANS MUST have a better word than *schadenfreude* for what I'm feeling. In Game 4, LeBron scores a total of 8 points, hitting 3 of 11 shots and 2 of 4 free throws. Not only is it the worst game of his career, he vanishes exactly as he did against the Celtics in Game 5 last season, drifting away from the action, unmoored from the game going on around him. In the entire fourth quarter, with the game up for grabs, he attempts one shot, and the Heat lose, 86–83.

Now the series is tied 2–2, with Game 5 coming up in two days, and the one question on everyone's mind is, What the hell is wrong with LeBron James?

HISTORY REPEATS ITSELF off the court as well: on the morning of Game 5, Stephen A. Smith and Chris Broussard are chatting on ESPN2 when Smith alludes to rumors he's heard about LeBron's on-court performance being affected by off-court matters "of a personal nature" involving "someone other than the player." Smith primly assures Broussard—who clearly knows exactly what Smith is referring to—that he would not reveal any details even if he could confirm said details, because they have "nothing to do with the game of basketball."

Soon the interwebs are ablaze with the story of LeBron's girlfriend's affair with Rashard Lewis, who plays for the Orlando Magic. Lewis, recently engaged to be married, quickly denies any such thing.

Months ago, when I began trying to find out if there was any truth to the Gloria James–Delonte West story, an NBA reporter suggested that one source of those rumors was none other than Maverick Carter himself, trying to deflect the blame for James's poor play against the Celtics. This sort of smut, two seasons running, seems far too strange to be a coincidence.

WHEN JAMES AND WADE enter the arena before Game 5, they're caught on camera coughing and laughing behind their hands, making fun of Dirk Nowitzki, who played with the flu during Game 4. It is an exceedingly bizarre moment in a Finals that has become a recurring nightmare for LeBron James.

Maybe it's because Wade dressed him down in Game 3 in front of millions of fans and both teams. Maybe it's because James is suffering from another of the undisclosed playoff maladies that befell him as a Cavalier. Maybe it's because Dallas coach Rick Carlisle, who was coaching the Indiana Pacers back when LeBron was a rookie being gelded by Ron Artest, is running Shawn Marion and DeShawn Stevenson at him like me and Big George at a cigarette machine. Whatever the reason, James is fading into nothingness game after game.

Nowitzki, meanwhile, dogged his whole career as a player who failed in the clutch, knows that this may well be his last chance to win a championship; the idea that he is faking an illness, as Wade and James seem to be suggesting, is insane. The Wade-James clown act mocking Nowitzki is emblematic of what the Heat have become: a genuinely loathsome team, flexing and roaring and beating their chests when they're ahead, panicking when they're pressured, and ref baiting on almost every offensive possession. They're preening, gutless chumps whose confidence seems more and more like delusion.

After Game 5—after Nowitzki scores 29 points and the Mavericks finish with a 17–4 run; after LeBron falls apart yet again in the fourth quarter, scoring 2 points; after Dallas rolls to a 112–103 win, pushing Miami to the brink of extinction—an irate Wade claims that his pregame coughing was genuine, while LeBron feebly attempts to deny that he's collapsing under the pressure of the Finals.

"I don't think so," he says.

"I don't believe so," he says.

"I know I'm not," he says.

· · ·

THE BOY, *KINEHORA*, is back in school and I'm cleared for takeoff. First-class both ways and all the way. I'm not staying across from Big Pink; I'm at the Viceroy. No Malibu; I'm rolling a Lincoln. No Luna Bars; I'll take the prawn salad for starters, and the ribeye.

I'm representing, motherfucker. I'm in Miami with every Cleveland fan who ever lived. I'm here with Manny and Lorry and Cousin Jeff. I'm here with my old man and his, and I've brought the thing on my nose for Lucille.

I'm here for Dan Gilbert and Mo fucking Williams, too. For Joe Gabriele. For Ray Chapman and Brian Sipe. For Walt Wesley, Dick Snyder, Jim Chones, and Joe Tait.

I'm here for Lisa, for Judah, and for the dog, who asked me to put five large on the Heat for him. I tend to agree.

Oh, yeah: I'm here for Nicky, too. And for that fat twelve-year-old kid who rides with me always.

I FIND A couple of tickets on the Heat's own website— because FanUp! in Miami means even the season-ticket holders would rather pocket a few bucks than watch the team fight for its life—in the lower bowl, near the Dallas bench.

My buddy Don Van Natta, a *New York Times* reporter who lives in Miami, is coming along to help keep me out of jail or the hospital in case things go even worse than I expect.

What do I expect? Let's put it this way: Game 6 is tonight, June 12. My return flight is the early bird on June 15—because Game 7 will be played on the fourteenth, and because the fifteenth is Judah's twelfth birthday. *Kine-hora*.

What I expect, as a lifelong Jew and Cleveland fan, is that the Whore of Akron will play the two most spectacular games of his career and forever etch his scoundrel's name into the history books.

What I expect is the usual. The Blue Ball Special: travail, with a side of woe and a big slice of rue for dessert.

I REMOVE THE white slipcover from the back of my chair, mop my brow with it, and stick it in my pocket. No need of it here: we are sitting in a sea of Maverick blue, and not the only one, not by a long shot. A quarter or more of the lower bowl is filled with Dallas fans.

Here the Whore of Akron chose to come, and here is where he belongs. He came of age in Northeast Ohio rooting for the fucking Yankees, the Dallas Cowboys, and Michael Jordan, and he has found a perfect place to play, where there is no home and there are no fans.

· · ·

HE OPENS BY hitting two 3-pointers.

"Uh oh," Van Natta says.

Nah. It's a good thing. He'll keep shooting jumpers.

Sure enough, he does. What worries me most—that he will suddenly remember he's LeBron James, that no one on the court can stop him—isn't happening. It isn't *going* to happen. His shots stop falling, and, once again, James stops playing.

Nowitzki misses jumper after jumper, but the Mavericks, playing with the sort of certainty I've never seen in a Cleveland playoff team, storm ahead by 12 points.

Then the Heat launch a 14-point run, and there's a scuffle down by the Heat bench. The Heat fans awaken at last. Some of them. A few of them. I can hear them at the other end of the arena, faintly. And back come the Mavs. Even with Nowitzki shooting 1–11, Dallas has a 2-point lead at halftime—because Jason Terry, LeBron's man on defense, has 19 points on 8–10 shooting. James, after scoring 9 points in the first 5 minutes, scores only 2 more the entire half.

LEBRON DOESN'T SCORE in the second half until under two minutes remain in the third quarter and the

Mavericks are ahead for good. He doesn't want to shoot, doesn't want to drive, doesn't even want the ball. As soon as it hits his hands, it's gone. In the last game of the season, fighting against elimination in the Finals, LeBron James's signature play is a quick swing pass to Juwan Howard.

When time mercifully runs out, he's still in a daze. He finds Dwyane Wade and hugs him for a long time. He drifts into the scrum of players and coaches shaking hands, stops and turns and leaves the court, head down. It's over.

I'M IN A state of serious confusion. Van Natta kindly gives me the tweet of a lifetime—"Not one"—and I text the boy ("Someday you and I will go to a game like this"), but I can't quite handle the emotional calculus.

There is no Cleveland laundry here, and yet I'm happier than I have been at a Cleveland game since 1964, and I feel no shame for that. LeBron James has lost in the worst possible way and I was here to see it.

But there's sadness, too.

"Not one" is still the same number of championships two generations of Cleveland fans have ever known.

FOR MOST OF seven seasons, I pulled hard for the kid. I rooted for him to succeed and he failed. Now I've

spent a year rooting for him to fail—and at failure, he suc-
ceeded beyond anything I could've hoped. It wasn't luck
or Mo Williams. It wasn't an injury or a lousy call at a key
moment. It was him. All him.

Now he's on the TV. Van Natta and I are at Tobacco
Road, an old Miami dive. Don's drinking light beer, the
point of which I've never understood. I'm drinking club
soda. The place is mostly empty, and nobody's looking at
LeBron on the TV but Van Natta and me.

Someone asks about how he feels about all the folks
rooting against him.

"At the end of the day they have to wake up tomorrow and have the same life they had before. They have
the same personal problems they had today. I'm going to
continue to live the way I want to live and continue to do
the things I want with me and my family and be happy
with that."

WAS IT EASY, LEBRON? Did it go down smooth
and sweet as peach cobbler? I almost feel bad for you, son.
You're not a grown man. You're a kid and you're afraid.

What are you so afraid of, LeBron, the losing or the
winning?

Do you finally understand that it's not easy? That it's
not meant to be easy. Hard is the only thing that makes it
mean anything, the only thing that makes losing or win-

ning worth the pain of trying, the only thing that makes living and dying worth the suffering.

Akron never taught you that. Nobody there loved you—not your talent, not your future earnings—loved *you* enough to teach you that there was suffering yet to come that no amount of money or talent could forestall forever. You had no father to teach you that a man doesn't give up and walk away, doesn't point his finger anywhere but at himself. You had nobody honest or smart enough to tell you that you can take your talents to South Beach, but that those innumerable talents don't travel alone—the demons come, too.

Learn to face those motherfuckers down, son, and you just might grow up to be a man someday.

ME, I'LL WAKE up tomorrow and point that rented Lincoln toward the airport. I'll turn on the radio and laugh out loud when I hear Le Batard talk about Pat Riley maybe shipping you to Orlando for Dwight Howard. They don't give a shit about you here, pal. You don't have a home team anymore. You never will.

I'll land at Terminal C in Newark, and Lisa will meet me and we'll head home. She'll wrap my swollen legs, and if the boy's still in school, we'll have time for some loving contemplation. The dog will be grateful I never placed the bet. The boy will smile and hug me when he sees me, and his smile and hug will push all that suffering to come a little farther into the far corner where history waits.

Let it wait. Great cities and great athletes live and die. No twelve-year-old can know that; I know it now. I see them pass like the seasons, quicker each year while I wait, too, like all Cleveland fans. Certain only of defeat, we wait.

Our love is our hope: that we'll somehow last long enough to witness that parade down Euclid Avenue, and that this—finally, always—could be the year.

ACKNOWLEDGMENTS

THANKS FIRST TO the journos who lit the way: Brian Windhorst, Bill Reiter, Jason Lloyd, Tom Withers, Joe Goodman, Dan Le Batard, Zac Jackson, Vince Grzegorek, John Krolik, Howard Beck, Jonathan Abrams, Adrian Wojnarowski, Chris Ballard, Buzz Bissinger, Wright Thompson, Surya Fernandez, and Andy Baskin.

To Don Van Natta Jr., Robin Thompson, and NFN Kalyan for help and inspiration in Miami; to Nicole Prowell, and Nathaniel Friedman, Jimmy Izrael, Brian Spaeth, and Joe Posnanski for creative kinship; to Jay Crawford for being a mensch; to Tim Livingston for transcribing.

To die-hard friends: Jeff Friedman, Jack Sanders, Sean Manning, Howard and Ken Elinsky, Joey Blackstone, Bryan Wessling, Ryan Coakley, Jon Frank, James Waltz, and Jay Woodruff.

To the Cavaliers organization, particularly Dan Gilbert, Tad Carper, Amanda Petrak, Tora Vinci, Mark Po-dolak, Chris Lesko, Garin Narain, and—above all—Joe Gabriele.

To Arnie Jensky, with deep gratitude.

To my *Esquire* family, with special thanks to Mark Warren, Eric Gillin, and Matt Sullivan; to Tom Junod, Tom Chiarella, and Cal Fussman; and with love to the man who made my career come true, David Granger.

This book would not exist if not for the hard work and tireless support of my friend and agent, David Black, and my friend and editor, the amazing David Hirshey. And it would not be the book it is if not for the brotherhood of Hirshey's protégé, Barry Harbaugh.

To Lisa Brennan, my soul mate and wife, whose unflagging patience, devotion, inspiration, and love are beyond words, I offer my heart. It has belonged to you since the day we met, and it always will.

ABOUT THE AUTHOR

Scott Raab, a Writer-at-Large for *Esquire* since 1997, is a graduate of Cleveland State University and the Iowa Writers' Workshop. His work has been widely anthologized, including in *The Best American Sports Writing*. Born and bred in Cleveland, he now lives in Glen Ridge, New Jersey. This is his first book.